CU00648735

WHITE STAR PUBLISHERS

## CONTENTS

HISTORY AND TREASURES OF AN ANCIENT CIVILIZATION

**TEXTS**
*NICOLETTA CELLI*

**EDITORIAL DIRECTOR**
*VALERIA MANFERTO DE FABIANIS*

**COLLABORATING EDITORS**
*LAURA ACCOMAZZO*
*GIORGIO FERRERO*

**GRAPHIC DESIGNER**
*PAOLA PIACCO*

**GRAPHIC LAYOUT**
*STEFANIA COSTANZO*

© 2009 White Star S.p.A.
Via Candido Sassone, 22/24
13100 Vercelli, Italy
www.whitestar.it

TRANSLATION: RICHARD PIERCE

ISBN 978-88-544-0407-6

Reprints: 1 2 3 4 5 6    13 12 11 10 09

Color separation: areagroup media, milan
Printed in China

1 - This gilded fret-worked wooden panel with a glass ground comes from the Wat Phra That Haripunchai of Lamphun.

2-3 - The *Ramakien*, the Tai version of the Indian epic poem *Ramayana*, is painted on the walls of the portico of the Wat Phra Kaeo in Bangkok.

4-5 - The gleaming pinnacles of the reliquaries in the Wat Phra Kaeo complex stand out in the heart of Bangkok.

6 - This statue of Buddha is a fine example of Dvaravati art (National Museum, Bangkok).

# INTRODUCTION

Of all the countries in Southeast Asia, Thailand has the most vibrant and well-chronicled cultural history. It is distinguished by many different cultural legacies that have been left by the many settlers – the Mon, Khmer and Tai – who have alternated, overlapped and finally merged into an original composite combination that is known as 'Thai' art and culture. The term 'Tai' refers to a group of related languages and, by extension, to the populations of Southeast Asia that speak these languages and share similar cultural traditions. Thai, or Siamese, belongs to this group and is now the national language of Thailand. This modern language is derived partly from the Tai population, which at the beginning of the 2nd millennium, had settled in the central plains of the country. This area was known among the neighboring populations as 'Syam,' hence the term 'Siam' that, since the late 13th century, has been used to refer, in a political context, to the Tais of the Kingdom of Sukhothai. The name 'Siam' was used up to 1939, when it was replaced by 'Thailand.' The new term better indicates the present territorial extension, which is greater than that of the ancient kingdom, and underscores the specific nature of 'Thai' culture. As mentioned, this new culture is the result of the long process of interaction between the settler-groups of Tais and the more ancient Mon and Khmer populations. The signs of these constituents can be seen in the richness and variety of Thai artistic production. During each period a new element came to the fore promoting different characteristics, inspiration and components, which are indeed so varied that at first sight they seem to stress change rather than continuity. In reality, like the many tesserae of a mosaic, all these constituents, each one totally different, create a complete portrayal of the multiethnic nature of Thai culture: they each represent various moments on a path of cultural growth that led the birth of modern Thailand. This new awareness of their composite cultural identity was acquired by the Thais no earlier than the 20th century and was symbolically marked by the name change of the country: ancient Siam became modern Thailand. Historically, Thailand's initial cultural outlook was linked with the arrival of the new Tai populations and the artistic and cultural ferment that accompanied them. This was subsequently replaced by a broader view that encompasses the more distant past and un-

derscores its continuity with the present. In the context of this new concept, which favors the study of all of the components that have contributed to the formation of 'Thai' identity, the history of the art of this nation has also changed its perspective. While Thai artistic development was once identified with the foundation of the kingdom of Ayutthaya, which marked the first important unification of the country, today the divide between the art that preceded and the art that followed the arrival of the Tai populations is obsolete. Nowadays, scholars prefer to concentrate on the origin and development of the motifs, styles and iconographies that permeate Thai history. They look at the new styles that have appeared as well as those that have been eradicated and study the changes and transitions that have occurred during each significant period. The process of cultural unification, which began in the 13th century with the contribution of the Tai – an operation that should not be underestimated – entailed the assimilation and selection of preceding traditions, especially those of the Mon and Khmer, which indeed are the most ancient roots of Thai civilization. In a later period, influences deriving from more recent contact with neighboring populations, as well as with Western culture, added new ingredients to the cultural amalgam that distinguishes present-day Thailand. In such a multifaceted panorama, it therefore seemed necessary – in consideration of what has been achieved since the first studies of this country were carried out – to consider the nature and characteristics of each of these traditions, investigating their rise and development, sources of inspiration, expressive modes and reciprocal influences. At the same time, we have not lost sight of the elements of continuity that have cropped up in different periods, contexts and regions. Beneath the new innovations lies a common substratum. The impact of this layer of aesthetic consistency has varied in intensity and significance but has contributed much in connecting all the diverse artistic experiences together. The first important factor of cohesion and cultural continuity was certainly Buddhism, which, despite the presence of other traditions and of a very strong indigenous religion, became the most widespread faith in the country. Hinduism, on the other hand, was less significant in this respect. Its rituals lay at the base of the royal ceremonies that

9 - THIS STATUE OF VISHNU (H. 4 FT 10 IN/148 CM) FOUND AT DONG SI MAHAPHOT IS WEARING THE CHARACTERISTIC CYLINDRICAL MITER DERIVED FROM INDIAN ICONOGRAPHY (NATIONAL MUSEUM, PRACHINBURI).

were performed by the Khmer and later inherited by the Thai kings. However, the government of the latter both promoted and supported the Buddhist doctrine and the monastic communities. From an artistic standpoint, there is no lack of evidence of the close bond that exists between one period of culture and another. This can be seen in the consistency of using certain materials, the use of architectural decoration – present from the Dvaravati up to the Sukhothai and Ayutthaya periods – or the preference for bronze sculptures and tiny bricks in architectural structures. The persistence of certain cultural models is evident in the geometric conception of space that prevails in the Khmer sanctuaries. This was transmitted to the sacred temple complexes of Ayutthaya and, also in the Angkor building of the *prasat*. This model subsequently became the *prang,* via the mediation of Lopburi art. Sculptures, as well certain other felicitous iconographic inventions, originating in the art of the Dvaravati kingdom – such as the seated Buddha protected by the *naga* – cropped up in later periods. These icons were then enriched with complex symbolism, as seen in the statuary of Lopburi, in Khmer sculpture and in the art of Ayutthaya. If, on the one hand these constant features allow us to follow the transmission of motifs, styles and techniques through Thailand's cultural melting pot, on the other there is no doubt that each era was marked by highly original aesthetic research of its very own. Far from being a vague and distant memory of the fascination and vigor of Indian art, the Thai works offer examples, many of which are sheer masterpieces, of well-pondered variations on already-known themes that are, however, transfigured by a new and powerful vision. The revival of forms, architecture and decoration with exquisitely elegant results seems to be the essence of the Thai aesthetic, from its very beginnings right up to the most recent Siamese art. Over the centuries, the signifiers of this aesthetic were the intense bronze Buddhas created in Dvaravati art, the magical architecture of the Khmer sanctuaries, which anticipate the perfection later achieved at Angkor, and the ineffable sculptures of the Sukhothai kingdom. Together with the solemn Ayutthaya monasteries and the elegant wooden artworks of Lan Na, these represent the spirit of Thai artistic endeavors. And even in Bangkok, where the redundancy and eclecticism of more recent centuries might appear to herald an art in decline, we can find, among the arts that have flourished in the new capital of Thailand, the ancient grace and splendor. This can be seen in the bejeweled statues, the mother-of-pearl 'frescoes' and the elegantly decorated lacquered panels.

10-11 - A painting in Wat Yai Suwannaram, Phetchaburi, depicting a Brahma worshipping.

14-15 - Brilliant demons made of colored glass guard the sanctuary towers inside the Wat Phra Kaeo complex in Bangkok and also serve as atlases for the bases.

16-17 - Wat Mahathat at Sukhothai includes many *chedi, wihan, mondop* and other secondary structures that are arranged around the main axis of this sanctuary.

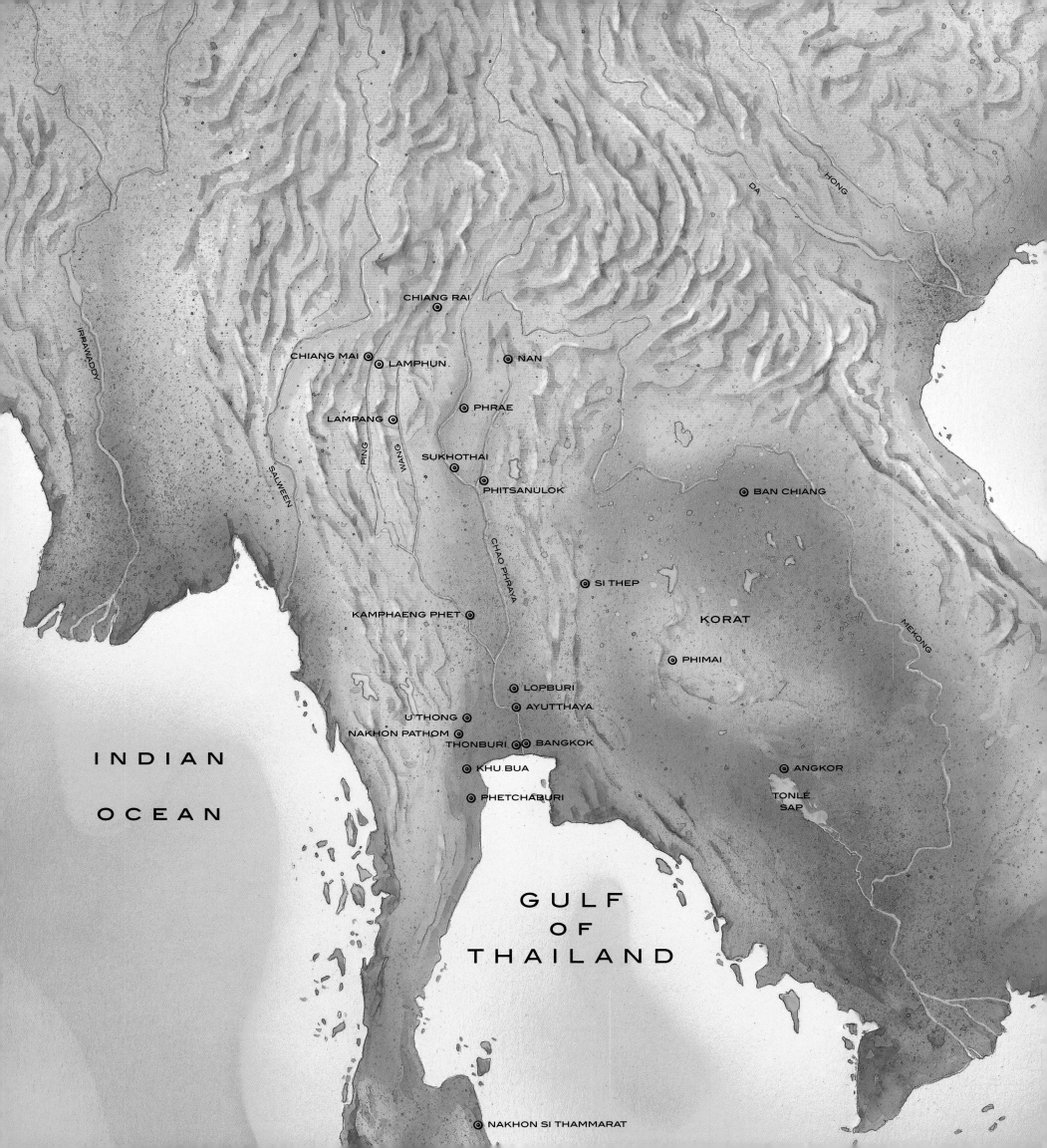

CHIANG RAI

CHIANG MAI ◎ ◎ LAMPHUN                ◎ NAN

LAMPANG ◎                ◎ PHRAE

                    SUKHOTHAI ◎
                        ◎ PHITSANULOK                    ◎ BAN CHIANG

PING
WANG

CHAO PHRAYA

                        ◎ SI THEP

KAMPHAENG PHET ◎                        KORAT

IRRAWADDY

SALWEEN

                                ◎ PHIMAI

                        ◎ LOPBURI
                        ◎ AYUTTHAYA

U THONG ◎
NAKHON PATHOM ◎
THONBURI ◎◎ BANGKOK                        ◎ ANGKOR

                                TONLÉ
                                SAP

INDIAN

OCEAN                ◎ KHU BUA

                ◎ PHETCHABURI

MEKONG

DA        HONG

GULF
OF
THAILAND

◎ NAKHON SI THAMMARAT

### FROM THE NEOLITHIC TO DVARAVATI
(3rd millennium BC– 11th century AD)

The most ancient traces of Neolithic settlements in Thailand date back to 2300 BC and their creation was connected to the expansion of Austroasiatic populations (Mon and Khmer). The first civilization to be documented by archaeological digs, inscriptions and the writings of Chinese historians was that of the Mon of Dvaravati, which developed from the 6th to the 9th century AD in central Thailand. Unified from a cultural standpoint by the common adherence to Buddhist doctrine, the Dvaravati civilization is represented by remains of *stupas*, 'wheels of the law,' statues, architectural decoration, and inscriptions found in various localities such as Nakhon Pathom, U Thong, Lopburi and Si Thep. The existence and expansion of Dvaravati were checked on the one hand by the kingdom of Srivijaya, which between the 8th and 11th century occupied the southern section of the peninsula, and on the other hand by the slow but inexorable penetration of the Khmer in the eastern region that culminated in the control of much of the country from the 11th to the 12th century.

### THE KHMER IN THAILAND
(10th–13th century AD)

At the dawn of the 9th century the Khmer kingdom of Angkor lay in the heart of ancient Cambodia and a dynasty of Angkorian rulers had begun with King Jayavarman II (790-850). From northeastern Thailand, a hybrid zone in which the Mon and Khmer cultures converged, from the 10th century on the Angkorian sovereigns initiated a policy of expansion the led to the conquest of central Thailand and made Phimai and Lopburi the provincial capitals of the kingdom. It was also thanks to this latter city that aspects of the Khmer civilization were transmitted to Thai culture and art.

### THE TAI ERA
(13th–18th century AD)

With the appearance on the scene of the Tai populations in the first centuries of the 2nd millennium AD another major protagonist took part in the cultural synthesis that informs present-day Thailand. After the foundation of the *muang* of Sukhothai on the part of King Inddraditya, the kingdom prospered with his successor Rama Kamhaeng (1278-98). This ruler laid the foundation for cultural unity by means of the adoption of Theravada Buddhism as the state religion and the creation of a writing system for the Tai language, and through a policy of alliances and conquests he extended the Sukhothai sphere of influence to an area form southern Burma to Laos. However, the fragile political unity was shattered during the reign of his son Lo Thai. Ayutthaya, founded in 1350 by Prince U Thong, emerged as the new power center, and in less than a century the kings who ascended the throne conquered the ancient territory of Sukhothai and then moved on to capture Angkor and began aggressive action against the Burmese, a policy that in the long run proved to be fatal, as is borne out by the destruction of the city in 1767 at the hands of their enemies.

### THE HISTORY OF NORTH THAILAND
(8th–19th century AD)

Caught between the expansionist aims of the Khmer and the birth of the Tai kingdoms, the history of Haripunchai is the last remnant (from the 8th to the 13th century) of a Mon kingdom in Thailand. The birth of the Tai kingdom of Lan Na, founded by King Mangrai in 1296, put an end to the independence of Haripunchai and marked the beginning of Tai supremacy in the north. Mangrai built his new capital, Chiang Mai, in the middle of his kingdom, which he ruled until 1317. During the reign of King Tiloka in the second half

of the 15th century, the Tai kingdom in the north got the better of Ayutthaya led by King Trailok and then enjoyed a brief period of great prosperity and cultural ferment. In the 16th century, the resumption of rivalry with Ayutthaya and the clashes with the Burmese ended up exhausting the kingdom of the north, which was therefore subjugated several times by both of its enemies. Even after the liberation from Burmese hegemony, Lan Na enjoyed only a short period of independence, which was followed by the annexation to the Kingdom of Siam in the 19th century.

### THE CHAKRI DYNASTY
(18th–19th century AD)

After being sacked by the Burmese in 1767, the revival of Ayutthaya began with Taksin, a skillful strategist and the founder of Thonburi, the short-lived capital of the new Siam. Taksin's reign ended rapidly and tragically, and the scepter passed into the hands of Rama I, a ruler of noble blood who in 1782 moved his capital to the opposite bank of the Chao Phraya River and two years later consecrated the birth of Bangkok and the rebirth of the kingdom with the placement of the statue of the Emerald Buddha in the temple specially built for I, the Wat Phra Kaeo. Of all the kings who then ascended the throne in the early 19th century, special mention should be made of King Mongkut (Rama IV), who managed to keep Thailand independent during the period when the European nations were colonizing the other countries in Southeast Asia. This king, who was a refined scholar and lover of archaeology—as were his son Prince Damrong Rajanubhad and his grandson Prince Subhadradis Diskul—was wholly committed to safeguarding the ancient monuments and his policy was continued by his descendants. This contributed to the important cultural debate that led to the rediscovery of the various roots of Thai history, culture and art.

# FROM THE NEOLITHIC ERA TO THE DVARAVATI CIVILIZATION

# THE NEOLITHIC ERA

The distant past of the history of Thailand (known as Siam until 1939) began to emerge from the high ground on the Korat plateau in the middle of the last century thanks to some important discoveries that revealed the originality and complexity of the local cultures that had flourished during the Bronze Age and Iron Age. For a long time merely considered to be the geographic and cultural appendage of both China and India, Southeast Asia appeared to offer no attraction, and above all, no contribution to the study of prehistoric and proto-historic periods in South Asia. To the contrary, all the scholars' attention was directed towards the historic societies that appeared to have developed from the Indian civilization. This view of Thailand changed only recently, and these traces of prehistoric Indochinese societies are now considered to be a sign of independent cultural development worthy of being studied for its own specific nature. The most ancient traces of permanent human settlements and agricultural activity in Thailand date to 2300 BC. Their appearance has been related to the expansion of Austronesian populations (the Mon and Khmer), which migrated southwards from the valley of the Yangzi River in southern China, settling in the regions of Southeast Asia. This phase was marked by the numerous Neolithic cultures and represented in their ceramics. Among these, that of Ban Chiang, in the northern part of the Korat plateau, is probably one of the best known and appreciated. The discovery of this site, and of about one hundred others that are culturally related, has contributed more than any other to our

19 - Wheels of Dharma like this one (h. 59 in/1.5 m) date to the 7th century AD and testify to the development of the first Buddhist civilization in Thailand (Musée Guimet, Paris).

20 left - This vase (h. 8 in/21.3 cm) made in the early 2nd millennium BC is an example of the original forms and decoration of Ban Chiang ceramics (Smithsonian Institution, Washington).

knowledge of another aspect of the Neolithic era in this region. The information gleaned has shed light on Bronze Age development in Thailand. The finds include a great many ceramic artifacts that reveal a tradition that continued for no less than two millennia, and various bronze objects made with technology that, according to the most recent dates proposed by archeologists, appeared on the scene at around 1500 BC. The development of metallurgy, first with the production of bronze (1500-500 BC) and subsequently of iron (from 500 BC onwards), marked the transformation of the Neolithic settlements into more complex societies. They were exposed to trade relations with the outside world and to the fertile circulation of new ideas from India that arrived by way of maritime commerce. During the Iron Age crucial changes took place: iron was used to make tools, which in turn allowed the settlers to exploit the land and favored great improvements in rice cultivation; many villages rose up along the main rivers in Thailand, causing a considerable population increase and trade with China and India brought new materials and new knowledge into the country. These contacts did not have immediate consequences on the cultural scene of the time (for example, the artistic production of this period does not betray any Indian influences), but the way had been paved for communication with the subcontinent. Contact that would be maintained over the centuries to come, and, around the middle of the 1st millennium, the artistic seeds that had arrived from India began to be assimilated and elaborated upon.

20 RIGHT AND 21 LEFT - BRONZE BRACELETS SUCH AS THIS ONE REVEAL THE HIGH LEVELS ACHIEVED IN THE PRODUCTION OF METAL OBJECTS AND ORNAMENTS AT BAN CHIANG.

21 RIGHT - THE MEANDER DECORATION ON THIS VASE FROM BAN CHIANG (H. 6 IN/16.7 CM) IS SET OFF BY THE CONTRAST BETWEEN THE RED PAINTING AND THE WHITE SLIP (SMITHSONIAN INSTITUTION, WASHINGTON).

The name Suvarnabhumi, or 'Land of Gold,' was used in ancient Indian literature to refer to the zone between present-day Burma and southern Thailand, which from the first centuries of the modern era was the destination of the traders who traveled toward the coasts of Southeast Asia. As we have seen, the dawn of this era of commercial relations with India, China and the other nearby countries dates back to the 4th century BC but, during the first centuries of the modern era, this trade became more intense and its impact on the local situation changed considerably. After skirting the Bay of Bengal and the Gulf of Martaban, the Indian merchants went beyond the Three Pagodas Pass, the highway that from the west penetrated the heart of Thailand and, by following the course of the Kwae Noi river, arrived at the central plains. On the opposite side, along the road that connected the Mekong and Mun rivers, the way was used for goods coming from southern China, with which Thailand had long-lasting relations. However, these relations were not to be as important for the cultural history of the country as the relations with India. Little is known about the process of the diffusion of Indian culture in Southeast Asia, known as 'Indianization,' which took place in the first millennium of the modern era. This phenomenon affected not only the languages and writing systems of the subcontinent, but also its religious beliefs, mythology, concepts of royalty and artistic styles. In fact, the information garnered from inscriptions and literary sources attests to the spread of Indian culture around the 1st-2nd century AD, and archeologists have found artifacts of Indian origin with Buddhist-inspired decorative motifs. However, the artistic and architectural testimony connected to Buddhism dates back no earlier than the 7th century. While for the moment questions concerning the details of this diffusion – which was by no means

a peaceful process – remain clouded in mystery, the results of recent archeological research are now modifying the obsolete image of Thailand as a passive absorber of foreign cultural elements. The configuration of the ancient cultures that lived in the country before Indianization is now better defined thanks to information provided by various disciplines. Nowadays, there is general agreement in acknowledging the leading role that these cultures had in forming the cultural destiny of Thailand through a conscious choice of the elements that were assimilated, and often modified and adapted, into their cultural tradition. It is most likely that, after the first occasional journeys toward the peninsula, the Indian merchants set about organizing actual trade stations for their commerce in the coastal localities. Most of these had already been inhabited further back in time, and in some cases these settlements developed into small 'states' or 'kingdoms.' With the headway made in coastal navigation and the discovery of trans-isthmus routes, the peninsular area of Thailand played a major role in the network of trade and commerce that animated the beginning of the 1st millennium. The traded goods comprised items not only from the countries of southern Asia, but also from the Roman world. A good example of the advantages of this new route can be seen in the Isthmus of Kra, which is a little over 31 miles (50 kilometers) wide. This narrow passage allowed the navigators to transport their cargo from the Indian Ocean to the Gulf of Thailand by passing through a strip of land, thus avoiding the much longer journey through the Strait of Malacca. It is therefore not surprising that this natural meeting place, the peninsula, and in particular the isthmus area, yielded statues stemming from Indian sculpture of both Buddhist and Hindu inspiration, some of which were rather important in the development of local art.

23 - THIS 6TH-CENTURY BUDDHA IN MEDITATION (H. 104 CM) FROM CHAIYA IS ONE OF THE OLDEST IMAGES OF THE ENLIGHTENED ONE MADE IN THAILAND (NATIONAL MUSEUM, CHAIYA).

24 - An 8th-9th-century bronze statue from the Indo-Chinese peninsula representing a *bodhisattva* (h. 2 ft/63 cm) with soft, sensual forms derived from Indo-Javanese art (National Museum, Bangkok).

25 - This sculpture (h. 15 in/38 cm) is an example of the iconographic type found exclusively in the Mon art of Thailand. It depicts Buddha seated on a mythical animal accompanied by two attendants (National Museum, Bangkok).

At the end of the 19th century Dvaravati was nothing more than a name. Indeed, in 1884 the scholar Samuel Beal had reconstructed the Sanskrit word 'Dvaravati' from the place name 'Duoluobodi,' which had been mentioned in Chinese sources to indicate an area between Cambodia and Burma with which China had trade relations. Beal proposed linking this name to a 7th-century kingdom in central Thailand. His felicitous theory was only confirmed in 1943 by the discovery, at Nakhon Pathom near Bangkok, of two silver medals with the following inscription in Sanskrit: 'The meritorious act of the ruler of Dvaravati.' Since that time the discovery of other medals with the same inscription, as well as other archeological finds, have established not only the existence of the name, but above all the historical existence of the ancient kingdom, many aspects of which are still unknown. The very term 'kingdom' is nothing more than a convenient way of designating a reality that is better known through its artistic production than its political fabric, since it seems that Dvaravati did not have established boundaries, and perhaps not even a true capital. In order to understand the origin of the first Thai civilization, we must consider the new trade routes that developed in the continental region side-by-side with the maritime routes and the roads that had been used since the Iron Age. Initially these first linked the bordering areas and then spread further into more distant lands. Along the interior tracks that followed the course of the Mun and Pasak rivers and connected the central plains and the east plateau, the local traffic prospered and the old villages began to grow at the dawn of the new millennium. Around the 5th and 6th centuries, with the decline of Indian control over trade, there came a transformation in the ancient villages, which were inhabited – at least in the northern part of the peninsula and the central plains – by people who spoke the Mon language. These ancient inhabitants of Thailand, nourished by the culture that had arrived from India, organized themselves into more complex and articulate communities. From these emerged larger, more dominant towns, traces of which are to be found in the urban settlements of U Thong, Nakhon Pathom and Chansen in the central plains, and recently brought to light by archeologists. Called *mandalas* by some contemporary schol-

ars (from the Sanskrit word for 'circle'), the political entities that arose from this process were distinguished for their fluid structure, which was capable of expanding and contracting, depending on their relationships with the surrounding towns. The city that succeeded in asserting itself economically and in establishing relations with other neighboring groups would prevail over the latter until such time as the balance of power thus created was upset by a new, more powerful and prestigious rival capable of forging alliances in its favor. Thus it was that around the middle of first millennium, Dvaravati, which was one of these geo-political entities, began to emerge and ended up acquiring a predominant position in the 7th century.

According to a historical reconstruction recently proposed by scholars and experts, Dvaravati was a political organization with variable borders. It was able to attract other nearby 'states' thanks to its charisma and the capacity of its ruler to earn and maintain alliances with the bordering *mandalas*. What cannot yet be established for certain is whether Dvaravati was a single large *mandala* or rather consisted of a territory divided into small, adjacent *mandalas* that competed for supremacy. The vagueness of the data concerning the territorial extension, structure of the government, and even the composition of the social fabric, is compensated by the archeological discoveries made in over a dozen sites in the central plains. These have highlighted various similar elements that validate the supposition that a Dvaravati civilization actually existed, and was made up of Mon populations, spread across the Chao Phraya River basin, and expressed by a homogeneous artistic output. The commercial fortune of the *mandala* was made possible thanks to the control exerted over the communication routes that connected the sites in its sphere of influence. These were located in the central plains and northeastern areas, with Burma and Cambodia on one side and Laos and Yunnan on the other. But what really determined the political and cultural cohesion, and thus the power wielded over the neighboring areas, was their adherence to Buddhism. The universal character of this doctrine proved to be quite effective in cementing the existing bonds among the small components of the 'state' and in transforming Dvaravati into a Buddhist civilization whose heritage would have a major impact on the later history of this region. Buddhism, which spread from southern India and probably penetrated Thailand as early as the 3rd century AD, quickly took root and replaced the ancient ancestor-cult that lay at the base of the socio-religious structure of many South Asian populations. The limits to social cohesion imposed by a religion based on family ties were overcome by the unifying and universal concepts of the Buddhist doctrine, with which different and distant communities could identify themselves. Actual proof of religious practices date only from the 7th century and consist of inscriptions carved in the Pali language, in numerous stone and bronze images of Buddha, and in the remains of Buddhist monuments. From that period onwards, these were built by the local elite groups in support of the foreign doctrine. Artistic development therefore followed the stabilization of the religion by at least three or four centuries, and in the 7th century the time was ripe for the blossoming of local art, whose most illustrious symbol were the *dharmacakrastambha* – the stone pillars crowned by the Dharma wheel. The scholar Robert Brown has suggested that the distribution and arrangement of the pillars may in some way define the sphere of influence of Dvaravati: if this were this the case, the heart of the *mandala* would have been in the area between the lower course of the Chao Phraya River (Nakhon Pathom, U Thong) and the course of the Pasak River (Lopburi, Si Thep), where most of the *dharmacakra* were found. The most peripheral finds include Yala, at the southern tip of the peninsula, Muang Bon, along the upper course of the Chao Phraya, and, further east, Muang Sima.

Besides the presence of pillars with the wheel, other important indications concerning the diffusion of the Dvaravati civilization have been revealed by archeological research. This has allowed scholars to locate the characteristic oval track, common to the Mon sites in the central plains, even in the northern settlements of Lamphun (ancient Haripunchai) and Phrae, and in the easternmost part of the Korat plateau (Muang Fa Daet). Almost all of these have an irregular plan that is bounded by a single or double moat. Some, such as Nakhon Pathom and U Thong, are particularly extensive, so much so that they have been identified as true urban centers and considered in the past as possible sites of the capital of Dvaravati.

From what can be surmised from the inscriptions, the rather large population of these cities was engaged in both commercial and artisan activities. They were, by means of donations, the main source of support for the Buddhist community as well as the principal driving force behind the development of Buddhist art through the commissioning of statues and monuments. Other major sites are Pong Tuk, which has revealed traces of many Buddhist monuments; Khu Bua, known for its extraordinary stucco and terra cotta decorations; Lavo (ancient Lopburi), where 8th-century Buddhist images were found, including one of the famous 'wheels of the Law' and Si Thep, which has also yielded Hindu statues, as have the sites of Muang Phra Rot and Dong Si Mahosod in the Bang Pakong Valley.

This civilization developed from the end of the 6th century up to the 9th century, but since Chinese historical sources make no mention of Dvaravati from the 8th century onwards, we must assume that the kingdom was partly obscured by the growing prestige of the maritime power of Srivijaya. This was centered at Palembang, on the island of Sumatra, from where it exerted its control over the peninsular part of Thailand. The supremacy of Srivijaya over the stretch of sea between China and India, and over the appendix of Thai territory between the 8th and 11th centuries, connected the artistic output of the peninsula to that of the Sumatran power. During this brief period, new inspiration of Indian derivation was introduced into the peninsula. Later on, in around the 10th-11th centuries, the eastern sector of the country was overrun by the Khmer. Following that, in the 12th century, they conquered an even larger extent of territory. Although the social organization and independence of Dvaravati did not survive the Khmer conquest, its cultural heritage, especially the Buddhist one, which had slowly taken root in the central plains, was handed down to the later periods, thus helping to define the configuration and essence of present-day Thailand. Parallel to this development, in the north of the country there remained an island populated with Mon people, the kingdom of Haripunchai, which according to belief was founded in the late 8th or early 9th century by populations that came from Lopburi. There, to a certain degree, the memory of the Dvaravati tradition was preserved right up until the rise of the Thai in the 13th century.

27 - A FAMOUS BRONZE SCULPTURE OF BUDDHA (H. 5 FT 2 IN/160 CM), WHO IS PROTECTED BY A *NAGA* AND IS PERFORMING THE *BHUMISPARSAMUDRA* GESTURE. THE STATUE DATES FROM THE LATE 12TH OR THE 13TH CENTURY (NATIONAL MUSEUM, BANGKOK).

# THE WHEELS OF DHARMA

The cultural features of the Dvaravati civilization can be better clarified through its artistic production, which for the most part is represented by Buddhist sculpture, the best-known and most spectacular examples of which are the *dharmacakra* (the 'wheels of Dharma'), as well as the statues of Buddha. These large stone wheels, sculpted in relief on both sides, rest on a plinth carved out of the same piece of stone, and they once crowned stone columns, which were genuine monuments in themselves. The 'Wheels of the Law' were discovered for the first time in the second half of the 19th century, but their meaning and function were only ascertained more than 50 years after their discovery. These sculptures were found in central and peninsular Thailand, in particular, the Nakhon Pathom zone and other western sites (U Thong), and there are now more than forty specimens, whose sizes range from 26 to 77 inches (70 to 195 cm) in diameter. Thanks to an extraordinary discovery made at U Thong, where archeologists found the fragments (cubic blocks, statuettes of gazelles and deer, pieces of the column shaft) of the entire composition including the wheel, it was possible to reconstruct the original form of the monument. It consisted of a pillar surmounted by an abacus on which the wheel stood in a vertical position. On each of the four corners of the abacus, there were usually statuettes of deer that refer to the Buddha's first sermon in the Deer Park of Benares. On the stone base, which was the anchor of the wheel, so to speak, were the sculpted images of Brahmanic divinities connected to solar symbolism (which the wheel itself also referred to) such as Surya and Vishnu, or the auspicious figure of Sri, the goddess of prosperity. The idea implicit in these columns surmounted by the Wheel of the Law derived from India and refers to Buddha's first sermon, in which he set into motion the 'wheel of Dharma.' The correct identification of these large wheels and an

understanding of where they were positioned was brought to light through the decipherment of the inscriptions found on various fragments. The text, which is almost always in the Pali language, refers specifically to the Buddhist doctrine, thus making it clear that the large sculptures were nothing else but a symbol of the Dharma. The origin of these works is once again varied, and according to a recently formulated theory, the pillars of Dvaravati are a local reinterpretation of the famous inscribed pillar of Sarnath (3rd century BC), together with Khmer influences on the iconographic motifs that decorate the wheels. While they were originally considered to be the most ancient testimony of the spread of Buddhism in Southeast Asia, today we know for certain that the wheels date from the 7th to the 9th century and that, above and beyond their artistic value, they are important indicators of the spread of the Dvaravati civilization. They show that it probably extended its range to include the eastern plateau, where it seems that there were no columns with wheels. But in the area between the basins of the Mun and Chi rivers, archeologists found Mon inscriptions, Buddhist relief-sculpture, and carved images that suggest the influence of the Dvaravati civilization. However, the most original feature of the culture that developed on the eastern plateau are the stone steles decorated with scenes from the *jataka* (tales of the previous births of Buddha) or with images of the Enlightened One either making a double *vitarkamudra* (the teaching gesture) or seated in meditation. These monuments bear witness to the persistence of the ancient megalithic tradition and how it adapted to the needs of the more recent Buddhist tradition: the custom of elevating stones, which was an integral part of the local megalithic cults, continued even after the rise and spread of Buddhism, albeit in the new guise of steles, which may have served to mark out the holy area (*sima*).

28 - THIS LARGE WHEEL (H. 3 FT 5 IN/105 CM) AND STONE GAZELLE WERE PART OF THE SAME MONUMENT AND SYMBOLIZED BUDDHA'S FIRST SERMON IN THE DEER PARK NEAR BENARES (NATIONAL MUSEUM, BANGKOK).

29 - THE ICONOGRAPHY OF THE *DHARMACAKRA* INCLUDES VARIOUS SUBJECTS, SOME OF WHICH DERIVED FROM HINDU TRADITION. HERE WE SEE SURYA (H. 28 IN/72 CM), A SOLAR DIVINITY, WITH TWO LOTUS BLOSSOMS (NATIONAL MUSEUM, BANGKOK).

# BUDDHIST ARCHITECTURE AND SCULPTURE

There aren't any perfectly preserved Dvaravati monuments, but at Nakhon Pathom and U Thong there are traces of the *stupas* that were built there. The ruins and artifacts found at these sites, as well as the shape of the miniature votive *stupas* placed on clay tablets (*phra phim*), have allowed experts to create a probable reconstruction of the monuments. They are more likely to have stemmed from north Indian architecture rather than that of Amaravati, a major Buddhist city on the eastern coast of India that was the starting point for the merchants and missionaries who sailed toward Southeast Asia. There are two distinguishing characteristics of these northern Indian monuments: they feature globular shapes rather than a hemispheric shape for the body of the *stupa* and they have no square shrine or niche (*harmika*). Phra Pathom Chedi at Nakhon Pathom is known as the most ancient *stupa* in Thailand, but the original monument has been incorporated into the structure we see today, which dates from the 19th century. The history of the *stupa* at Nakhon Pathom bears witness to the custom, common to the entire Buddhist world, of restoring holy places and monuments – above all the *stupas*, which house especially popular relics – by covering the original monument with a new structure. The remains of Chedi Chula Pathom lie in the vicinity of Nakhon Pathom. Twentieth-century surveys of the ruins of the monument brought to light the brick foundations, which were hidden inside more recent reconstructions. The most ancient part consisted of the base of the *stupa*, dating from the 7th century, which was covered the following century by another level. Further additions were made to the *stupa*: it was rebuilt in the 8th century and stucco reliefs depicting the *jataka* were added, which are now kept in the National Museum of Nakhon Pathom. According to reconstruction work carried out by scholars, the shape of this monument was modeled on the Buddhist monuments found in Nalanda, in northeastern India. In particular, one of the most widespread designs in the 7th century had a tall, square or rectangular brick base with niches on each side that housed images of Buddha. Stucco sculp-

tures decorated the sides. However, other scholars state that Chedi Chula Pathom was inspired by southern Indian architecture. The other Dvaravati sites with *stupas* are Muang Bon and Khu Bua, respectively north and south of Nakhon Pathom. In the latter, archeologists found beautiful examples of terra cotta architectural decorations similar to the more ancient types found at Chedi Chula Pathom. The digs carried out at Pong Tuk and U Thong have, on the other hand, confirmed the presence of *stupas* with round, square or octagonal layouts, impressive rectangular mausoleums (*caityas*), and the foundations of ancient dwelling places (*viharas*). The reliefs that decorated and covered these monuments, some of which have been preserved, reveal the variety of Dvaravati art. Early examples are the terra cotta statuettes discovered at Khu Bua. With their soft modeling and delicately fashioned faces framed by rich headdresses or precious jewels, these figures, which are often more than 39 inches (one meter) tall, make up the compositions placed at the base of the monuments of *bodhisattvas* or enlightened beings surrounding Buddha. The sumptuous, sophisticated beauty of these images reminds one of the Gupta art of India, which is here masterfully and imaginatively elaborated by the artists of the local workshops. However, there are many more stucco works than terra cotta ones; indeed, most of the architectural decoration that has survived consists of the former. The small panels are made of stucco placed over a wood or bamboo armature, while in the case of larger compositions the armature may even be made of bricks or laterite. Created to animate the panels that formed the base of the monuments, these stucco compositions portray scenes of the former births of Buddha, mythical beings, animals and divinities. The examples that have been preserved manifest a rather varied artistic production that includes the panels of Khu Bua (sculpted around the 8th century), decorated with highly elegant figures depicted with a marked naturalism. In a similar vein, those of Chedi Chula Pathom of Nakhon Pathom (8th-9th centuries) were created with equal mastery and imagination.

30 - STUCCO FRAGMENTS SUCH AS THESE (H. 12 IN/31.5 CM) WERE PART OF COMPOSITIONS ILLUSTRATING THE FORMER BIRTHS OF BUDDHA OR EDIFYING STORIES OF BUDDHISM (NATIONAL MUSEUM, BANGKOK).

31 - THE DECORATION OF THE DVARAVATI RELIGIOUS MONUMENTS WERE MADE OF STUCCO, AS CAN BE SEEN BY THIS HEAD (H. 7 IN/17 CM) OF A SEMI-DIVINE BEING (MUSÉE GUIMET, PARIS).

Without a doubt the material most used in Thai sculpture, from the Dvaravati period onwards, was bronze, a material with which the sculptors attained outstanding results. Their works are unsurpassed for quality and technical perfection by the other artistic schools of south Asia. The Dvaravati statues, cast with the lost wax (*cire perdue*) technique, are hollow when large and made of solid bronze when small. This metal was predominantly used because it lasts much longer than other materials. However, we must also bear in mind that, with the exception of calcareous schist and sandstone, which is available only in the eastern area, Thailand does not have much stone suitable for sculpture work. Despite the friable nature of schist, the Dvaravati sculptors succeeded in creating works of great beauty and originality thanks to certain methods that became the stylistic requisites of their school. Probably the most representative image of Dvaravati sculpture is that of the standing Buddha. Statues of this type, both in bronze or stone, were sculpted from the 7th century on and are always rigorously frontal. These works abide by a principle of symmetry that governs not only the gestures – almost invariably the *vitarkamudra*, which is made with both hands on a level with the chest – but also the arrangement of the cloak, which covers both shoulders and descends on either side with an equal number of folds. The monastic cloak, adhering perfectly to the body, heightens the asexual anatomy; the round face with the pronounced nose, the characteristic triple-arced curve of the joined eyebrows and the fleshy lips are the most distinguishing features of the Dvaravati-style images of Buddha. His hair, with its large curls covering the truncated cone-shaped cranial protuberance (*usnisa*), is another major feature. The stylistic origin of this figure is still a moot question among art historians, who have from time to time indicated and theorized about differing local influences. Without excluding other influences, mention should be made of the sculpture of Sarnath (near present-day Benares, in India), with which the Dvaravati type of Buddha is markedly similar in certain respects. This similarity occurs in the facial features, the *usnisa*, the type of hairstyle, the folds of the neck, the rendering of the adherent clothing, and the same lack of representation of the *urna*. Leaving aside the various implicit influences, the Dvaravati Buddha is a highly original creation, especially regarding the gesture of the double *vitarkamudra*, which became widespread in the sculptural schools of later periods. Besides the work described above, there are other famous standing figures that are exceptions to the typical symmetry and that depict Buddha with his right shoulder covered and his hands in various positions: for example, the right hand making the *vitarkamudra* or *varadamudra* gesture, while the left one is holding the hem of his robe. The images of the seated Buddha, in the *pralambapadasana* (that is, seated in the Western manner) or *virasana* (with his legs crossed and only the sole of the right foot visible) variations, are far rarer. As for the former position, it is repeatedly demonstrated in certain terra cotta votive tablets and in the colossal images made of quartzite that can be found at Nakhon Pathom. These show the Enlightened One with both hands making the *vitarkamudra* gesture, but not in a symmetrical position. The statues, sculpted in a material that is much more resistant then limestone but much more difficult to carve, create an effect of grandiosity and stateliness, even though it is possible to see that the sculptor struggled when working on the different planes.

32 - This terra cotta Buddha with pronounced features is seated in the *pralambapadasana* position. Similar images decorated the Dvaravati *stupas* (National Museum, Bangkok).

33 - The well-defined oval shape of the face, triple arch described by the eyebrows, and full lips are the characteristic features of the Dvaravati Buddhas (Musée Guimet, Paris).

*2*

# THE KHMER IN THAILAND

The Mun River basin, in the heart of the Korat plateau, boasts the greatest concentration of Khmer temples built outside Cambodia. Here Khmer expansion began in the 6th century, initiating a new chapter in the history of Thailand that was rich in cultural and artistic achievement, some of which have survived to the present day. The Mon population, which settled in the central plains, and the Khmer, who settled along the lower course of the Mekong River, shared a common past from a linguistic and cultural standpoint, a heritage that accompanied them to the end of the first millennium AD. Both the Mon and Khmer ethnic groups were part of the Austronesian populations that migrated south to the regions of South China. In more recent epochs, a few centuries before the Christian era, the differences between the two

Angkor, the 'holy city' or 'capital,' was the center of a powerful *mandala* that exerted wide-ranging control over the area around the median course of the Mekong. It became part of the continental territory of Southeast Asia from the 11th century onward. Northeastern Thailand was already governed by Khmer rulers before the reforms enacted by Jayavarman II (802-835), but essentially he was the king who created Angkorian political power using the foundations that had been laid for the birth of a centralized state. Inscriptions in Sanskrit and ancient Khmer that were found at the confluence of the Mun and Mekong rivers narrate the Khmer victories in this area, and the ruins of the 7th-century temples document the rituals organized by the kings in order to sanction their authority over that territory. The 10th century, dur-

groups prevailed over their ancient, common heritage: two different languages developed (Mon and Khmer) and, later on, in the basins of the Chao Phraya and Mekong rivers, the power centers that would mark the history of the two areas (Dvaravati and Angkor) began to take shape. While Buddhism became the pivotal point of reference for the Mon of Dvaravati, the gods of Hinduism populated the religious universe of the Khmer. Although they are partly sheathed in mystery, the origins of the Angkor civilization can be traced to the area of Zhenla, along the median course of the Mekong. This area is where, from the mid-6th century up to the early-9th century, various political states were engaged in a power struggle. Side by side with the birth and development of the *mandala* of Dvaravati in the heart of Thailand, the territory of present-day Cambodia witnessed the development of the conditions necessary for the formation of the Khmer kingdom of Angkor, which lasted from the 9th to the 13th century.

ing the Angkorian supremacy, witnessed the beginning of actual military expansion westward, which in the following two centuries ensured Cambodian control of almost all of Thailand, except for the northern and peninsular areas of the country. For a *mandala* like Angkor, which had a strongly knit and centralized organization and was economically powerful thanks to the abundant rice harvests resulting from a particularly advanced water control and irrigation system, the conquest of Dvaravati, which had extremely different characteristics, was unproblematic for the Khmer. Their expansion began from the area surrounding the Donrek mountain range, which formed a natural border, and then proceeded westward between the 11th and 12th centuries to the Korat plateau and the Lopburi area, in the heart of Thailand. Their attempt to occupy the northern regions, where the longest-ruling Mon kingdom, that of Haripunchai, still reigned, resulted in the defeat of the Khmer and the end of this initiative.

34 - IN THE ART FROM LOPBURI BUDDHA IS DISTINGUISHED BY A MYSTERIOUS SMILE, THE BAND SEPARATING THE FOREHEAD AND THE HAIR, AND THE STYLIZED LOTUS SURROUNDING THE *USNISA* (NATIONAL MUSEUM, BANGKOK).

36 AND 37 - THE PHIMAI SANCTUARY IS AN EXAMPLE OF PROVINCIAL KHMER ART, THE INNOVATIONS OF WHICH WERE EXPORTED TO ANGKOR AND THEN PERFECTED AT ANGKOR WAT.

The most important provincial cities conquered by the Khmer were Phimai, situated along the Mun River, and Lopburi, in the Pasak River Valley. Built in the mid-11th century, or at the very latest at the beginning of the 12th century, on 8th to 9th-century foundations, the temple complex of Phimai is situated at the end of the main road, which is paved in laterite and connected Angkor to the administrative capital of the Khmer province. This artery is the best surviving example of the road network that linked the heart of the Angkorian Empire and the provinces. The system consisted of elevated roads that could be used even during the rainy and flood season. The roads crossed over waterways thanks to the many bridges, and Jayavarman VII (1181-1215) built over one hundred *dharmasala* along the roads; resting places for travelers, especially pilgrims. We can gather, from inscriptions, that the city of Phimai, which in more ancient times was known as Vimayapura, had a history that dates from the Iron Age. It grew in importance and, at the end of the 11th century, it became the seat of the royal sanctuary of Jayavarman VI (1080-1107). The house of this ruler, known as the Mahidharapura dynasty, probably originated in this area of Thailand and appeared to have no connection with the family line that ruled Angkor. There is plausible proof of this in the inscriptions that specifically mention the king's lineage, which were found at Prasat Phnom Wan, a temple situated a few kilometers west of Phimai. The concentration of temples in eastern Thailand during this period may well indicate a special relationship between sanctuaries and the Khmer sovereigns who came from this region. It also implies a shift of the power center from Angkor to the provinces. However, many facts remain in obscurity and this makes it difficult to fully understand the relationship between Jayavarman VI and the capital of the Khmer empire, which it seems the king never used as his residence. Furthermore, Jayavarman VI was the first Khmer ruler (followed a century later by Jayavarman VII) to make Mahayana Buddhism the state religion. In doing this he laid the foundation for a combination of Buddhism and the cult of the god-king that the Khmer civilization later passed on to the Tai of Ayutthaya.

38-39 - THE GREY SANDSTONE OGIVE IN THE PHIMAI SANCTUARY STANDS OUT AMONG THE REMAINS OF THE OTHER RED SANDSTONE AND LATERITE STRUCTURES THAT CONSTITUTED THE RELIGIOUS CENTER OF THIS ANCIENT CITY.

The Khmer of Angkor elaborated many ideas from India, often in a more original manner than other populations. They created an ideology that allowed for the development and long-term duration of the Cambodian *mandala* (which lasted for no less than six centuries) and they profoundly fashioned the Angkorian civilization, which was given a constitution that was truly individual within the panorama of the cultures influenced by India in Southeast Asia. The concept of the divine nature of the king, which was mirrored in the elaborate investiture ritual as well as in the architecture and sculpture, was later transmitted to the Tai who replaced the Khmer in the Angkorian provinces and amalgamated it with Buddhist customs and thought. The impact of this heritage can still be seen in the ritual of Thai court ceremony, but above all in the organization of their living space and in religious architecture, as well as in some of the iconographic features in the images of Buddha. In the Khmer culture the administration of power was based on a particular cult, that of the *devaraja* (the god-king), which was established in the 9th centu-

ry and celebrated the identification between the king and the main god of Hinduism (usually Shiva). This link, sanctioned by a ceremony celebrated on a mountaintop, was also expressed by means of a stone phallic symbol, the *linga*, which was housed in the royal sanctuary in the middle of the city. This religious orientation of the Khmer sovereigns changed for a brief period during the reign of Jayavarman VI (at the end of the 11th century) and a second time in the final Angkorian phase (late 12th-early 13th century). During these times, Mahayana Buddhism replaced the Hindu religion, but it did not modify the concept of the divine nature of royalty or the symbolic concept of religious architecture. The constellation of temples remaining at Angkor bears witness to the role this city played as a religious center and theater for the rituals and ceremonies that guaranteed the continuity of the *mandala* and renewed the power of every king over the land. Built during the Angkorian period as the tangible abode of the *devaraja*, the temple structure evokes the center of the Universe as represented by the mythical Mount Meru.

40 - THE STATUE OF JAYAVARMAN VII (H. 4 FT 3 IN/132 CM) IS ONE OF THE MANY IMAGES THAT THIS RULER HAD PLACED IN VARIOUS TEMPLES IN HIS EMPIRE (NATIONAL MUSEUM, PHIMAI).

41 - IN THE MIDDLE OF A PEDIMENT IN THE PHIMAI SANCTUARY IS A RELIEF DEPICTING THE GOD SHIVA DOING HIS COSMIC DANCE MARKED BY THE MOVEMENT OF HIS TEN ARMS.

42 - THIS HEAD OF
BUDDHA, PART OF WHOSE
ORIGINAL GILDING HAS BEEN
PRESERVED, WAS CARVED
DURING THE LOPBURI
PERIOD (NATIONAL MUSEUM,
BANGKOK).

43 - BECAUSE OF THE
KHMER INFLUENCE, THE
IMAGE OF BUDDHA
PROTECTED BY THE *NAGA* (H.
6 FT/185 CM) ACQUIRED
SUCH EARTHLY SYMBOLS AS
A CROWN TO UNDERSCORE
THE ROYAL NATURE OF THE
ENLIGHTENED ONE
(NATIONAL MUSEUM,
BANGKOK).

44 - The lowered eyelids, faint smile and serene expression are characteristic features of the face of Buddha as depicted in 12th-13th century Angkorian art and in the art produced in Lopburi (National Museum, Bangkok).

Placed in the middle of the city, and hence in the middle of the *mandala*, the temple represents 'the abode of the gods,' the font of the Khmer world. To the Khmer, this was also seen as a manifestation of the center of the entire universe, and at the same time the guarantee of its very existence. This geometric concept of space gives rise to some important constants in Khmer architecture, such as the adoption of orderly plans for both the cities and temples, the interlinked arrangement of the constructions and the quincunx configuration of the sanctuaries in keeping with the temple-mountain style. This model of orderly space reappeared later in the Buddhist complex of Ayutthaya and can be clearly seen in the regular arrangement of its components: the quest for a harmonious relationship between the monuments, the primacy of the *prang* (the characteristic Siamese sanctuary tower) and the geometric principles that govern the internal configuration of the area. In a similar manner, through modifications made to one of the most long-lasting images in Thai art – the seated Buddha protected by a *naga* – one can note the superposition of the symbols of royalty and their passage from Angkor to Ayutthaya. This image, which probably drew inspiration from southern India (Amaravati) or Sri Lanka (Anuradhapura), first appeared in Dvaravati art in the form of a sculpted relief on votive steles. The scene refers to one of the episodes in the life of Buddha: when the king of the serpents (*nagaraja*) Mucilinda protected the Enlightened One from a storm with his hood while he was meditating. In Thailand, a 7th-8th century relief sculpture found at Dong Si Mahaphot, depicts the seated Buddha with his hands in the *dhyanamudra* position, while a many-headed cobra coils around his head, forming a sort of aureole. Other, similar statues were widespread in the 8th century in the vicinity of the lower course of the Mekong River, where the existence of a pre-Buddhistic serpent cult is likely to have favored the assimilation of images of the Enlightened One and the *naga*. Elaborated since the 11th century by Khmer artists, this sculpture of Buddha seated on the coils of a serpent, covered by cobra hoods spread to some degree in Thailand. It was prevalent at the beginning of the 12th century, during the time of Jayavarman VI, the ruler of Phimai who is associated with the figure of the god Vimaya. According to an interesting theory that was recently formulated, the representation of Vimaya is to be associated with the statue of the seated Buddha, decorated with jewels and protected by the *naga*. The choice of an image of Buddha bejeweled with royal insignia and protected by the serpent celebrating the divine

nature of the king is by no means foreign to Khmer conception. Both in pre-Angkorian mythology and in that of other Southeast Asian traditions, the origin of a dynasty was often traced back to the union between an ancestor and a *nagini*, that is, a serpent goddess. The figure of Buddha protected by the serpent and bestowed with royal attributes represents on the one hand the fusion of ancient local religion with Buddhism, and on the other an emphasis on the features of universal royalty developed by Mahayana Buddhism. In the images of Khmer derivation that were produced in Thailand in the 12th century, this attribute of royalty is underscored by the crown with bands and the earrings worn by the Enlightened One. These sculptures later led the artists of the Lopburi school to develop original and extremely ornamented creations, and from here this motif passed on to Ayutthaya art. However, in a later period the characteristic of royalty prevailed over the iconography of Buddha covered and protected by the *naga*. In fact, while the sculptors of Ayutthaya continued to produce images influenced to some degree by Khmer taste, this iconography was subject to changes due to the influence of the art of northeast India. The most important of these alterations was the substitution of the *dhyanamudra* with the *bhumisparsamudra*, the gesture referring to the invocation of the Earth as a witness of Buddha's enlightenment. The images depicting this position were particularly popular in northeast India, the region where Buddha attained enlightenment, in the locality of Bodhgaya. The iconographic image of Buddha seated with his right hand in the *bhumisparsamudra* position and wearing the royal attributes of a pointed crown and neckband, was one of the most widespread images in India and Burma in the 11th century. It was the latter country that passed it on to the Ayutthayan artists. Although the iconography of Buddha demonstrating the *bhumisparsamudra* gesture beneath the *naga* survived initially, a short time later, images of the ornate Buddha, either seated or standing, obscured the former image and finally replaced it completely. However, both were subject to innumerable stylistic variations by later sculptural schools. The primacy of the aspect of royalty over the former biographical references to Buddha was not a mere change in taste but rather reflected a more profound change that took shape in the 13th-14th centuries. This is revealed by the absence of images of the Enlightened One with royal attributes during the Sukhothai period and, vice versa, by their reappearance during the Ayutthaya period, coinciding with the formulation of the ideology of royalty in its purely Siamese form.

46 - BUDDHA DECORATED WITH ROYAL
INSIGNIAS AND SEATED IN MEDITATION WAS A
FAVORITE MOTIF OF PROVINCIAL KHMER ART,
WHERE IT WAS USED IN MANY VARIATIONS
(NATIONAL MUSEUM, BANGKOK).

47 - THE MODEL OF THE STANDING BUDDHA
MAKING THE DOUBLE *VITARKAMUDRA* GESTURE
TYPICAL OF DVARAVATI ART IS HERE ELABORATED
IN KEEPING WITH KHMER ICONOGRAPHY AND
TASTE (PRIVATE COLLECTION).

# THE PRINCIPALITY OF LOPBURI

Lopburi, which boasted an ancient history and was crucially important during the Dvaravati period, became part of the Khmer sphere of influence after the conquest of Suryavarman I in the early 11th century. It acquired a leading role in the 13th century, becoming Jayavarman VII's provincial capital, which was governed by one of the king's sons. For the entire 11th and 12th centuries the city attempted to free itself from Khmer dominion, until Jayavarman VII definitively placed it under the authority of Angkor. The rebellion of Lopburi, the most turbulent of the Khmer provinces, and the strong reaction of Haripunchai to the assaults undertaken by the Angkor Empire, epitomized the response of regions that felt themselves to be culturally distinct from the Cambodian world. The ancient Mon heritage of Dvaravati survived in Lopburi not only in the language, but also in the religion and social fabric, which consisted mostly of Tai populations, whose presence after the first millennium was destined to increase. For that matter, the Khmer were aware of the ethnocultural differences of this province. For them Lopburi was the administrative center of Siam, which was the region that provided Tai soldiers for conscription into the Khmer army. They were mentioned in an inscription and immortalized in the mid-12th century in the bas-relief sculpture at Angkor Wat, the Cambodian capital of the Khmers. The occasion to break free from Ankgorian rule arose at the end of the 13th century. The principality of Lopburi succeeded in declaring its independence and, albeit with a limited amount of political power, was able to enjoy a period of peace and autonomy, becoming one of the power centers in the eastern part of the central plains. It was at this crossroads of the various expressions of Thai culture that both Theravada and Mahayana Buddhism mixed with the Brahmanic concepts of the Khmer world, thus creating a unique religious and cultural syncretism. The importance of these different components would soon manifest itself, when Lopburi was incorporated into the Ayutthaya sphere of influence in the mid-14th century. A new order would be created from the two traditions inherited from the past: the Tai kings, formerly simple rulers who safeguarded the Law and the Buddhist community, were now cloaked in a new mystique thanks to the protection of the Brahmanic gods, guaranteed by the rituals that stemmed from the Khmers.

48-49 AND 50-51 - THE TAI TROOPS INCORPORATED INTO THE KHMER ARMY AS DEPICTED AT ANGKOR WAT WEAR JERKINS WITH FLORAL PATTERNS AND HEADDRESSES THAT ARE EITHER FEATHERED OR BIRD-SHAPED. THE FACES OF THE TAI SOLDIERS REVEAL THEIR DIFFERENT ETHNIC ORIGIN.

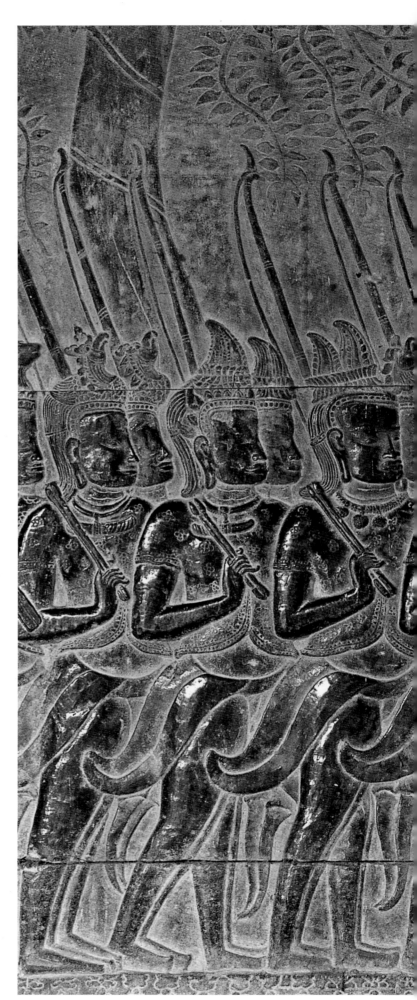

Testimony of the presence of the Khmer at Lopburi can be seen today at Phra Prang Sam Yot and Wat Phra Si Ratana Mahathat, surviving monuments that reflect the two different provincial traditions. One modeled on 12th-13th-century Angkorian architecture, and the other on the 12th-century Phimai style respectively. The former monument documents the form of the *prasat*, while the latter heralds that of the *prang*, the characteristic reliquary tower of Thai architecture that appears to be fully developed at Ayutthaya. The *prasat* is the characteristic temple of Khmer architecture. Its elementary structure consists of a cubic cella with a single entrance on one side and three false doors on the other sides. The projecting cornices of the false doors and the vigorously defined corner pillars add a touch of indentation to the square plan of the cella and animate the outer surfaces of the sanctuary with protuberances and recesses, including niches that contain the statues of semi-divinities. The roof is pyramid-shaped and comprises a series of superimposed levels of decreasing dimensions, each of which is a miniature reproduction of the decoration of the cella façade. The development of the *prasat* structure, in the form that was so widespread in the golden age of Angkorian architecture and heralded the birth of the *prang*, took place in the provinces, especially those of Phimai and Lopburi. The innovative influence of the former city can be seen in the fusion of the two elements of the *prasat*, the cella and its roof, in the upward thrust of the monument, which was now constructed on a tall platform, and in the ogives that gave the profile to the roof. This profile was set-off by the curve of the antefixes that rounded off the corners of the pyramid. On the other hand, it was probably at Lopburi that the ancient *prasat* was transformed into the reliquary tower, which would become the hallmark of Thai architecture. Although relations between Phimai, Lopburi and Ayutthaya and the transitions that led to the birth of the Siamese reliquary tower have yet to be clarified, the *prang* of Wat Phra Si Ratana Mahathat at Lopburi is generally considered to be the precursor of the *prangs* at

Ayutthaya. Phra Prang Sam Yot consists of three *prasats* connected to one another by roofed passageways. The model for this work was the tower in the late 12th-century *gopura* or entrance pavilion of Preah Khan at Angkor. The shape of the three *prasats*, whose roofs have square plans that are clearly distinguishable from the cella, has nothing of the tapering, continuous line of the *prasat* at Phimai. It also differs in the building materials: it is made of stuccoed laterite, which is a characteristic feature of most of the architecture constructed during the reign of Jayavarman VII. Wat Phra Si Ratana Mahathat, on the other hand, betrays the persistent influence of Phimai. There were two building phases for this complex: the first in the 12th century and the second in the late-13th century. It is thought that the latter period witnessed the construction of the sanctuary, which many scholars consider to be the archetype of the Thai *prang*. The model of the Phimai *prasat*, in which the cella and roof are perfectly integrated, is not only imitated here, but the elevation from the ground of the passage of the *mandapa*, was the basis for a totally new form. The monument of Lopburi consists of a cella with a roof made up of various levels that become progressively smaller as they rise. They reproduce, in miniature, features of the main façade of the sanctuary, as well as its denticular plan. The typical ogival profile, which distinguishes the Khmer *prasats* from the 12th century onward, seems well defined here, but the recessing of the various levels is less pronounced than in classical examples. The result is a surface that is smoother, not interrupted by the recesses of the roof levels, therefore it is a structure with marked verticality that anticipates later Siamese development. The tall platform and the four projectiles of the entrances, especially the eastern one, still belong to the Khmer style, as does the symmetrical decoration of the cella that is repeated on each roof. Therefore, it is possible to see how this model from Lopburi inspired the construction of the characteristic monument of Ayutthaya architecture, which was the hub of the great Buddhist monasteries of the time.

52 - PHRA PRANG SAM YOT AT LOPBURI CONSISTS OF THREE *PRASATS* AND WAS MODELED AFTER THE ENTRANCE TO THE PREAH KHAN, THE KHMER TEMPLE BUILT AT ANGKOR.

53 - THE FALSE DOORS OF THE *PRASAT* OF PHRA PRANG SAM YOT AT LOPBURI, WHICH ARE PROTUBERANT ELEMENTS OF THE BUILDINGS, MAKE THIS CELLA-SANCTUARY A CRUCIFORM STRUCTURE.

*3*

# THE TAI ERA

## SUKHOTHAI: THE 'DAWN OF HAPPINESS'

Around the year 1000 and in the following centuries, Thailand was divided between zones dominated by the Khmer, which comprised most of the country, and others occupied by the Mon from the kingdom of Haripunchai, who controlled the north-western territories. This was the context in which the numerous Tai populations appeared on the scene, populations that from re-mote times had moved from the southern regions of China (Yun-nan) toward the Chao Phraya and Mekong river basins. Despite the fact that this peaceful migration had begun a few centuries earlier, the phenomenon took on a certain degree of importance in around the 11th-12th centuries, when the presence of the Tai was not only clearly visible, but also brought about political changes that proved to be fundamental in the following centuries. Two centuries later, the crisis of the Khmer at Angkor and of the Burmese at Pagan had already set in. The enlargement of the canals along the borders of the empires and the weakening of the central power in the peripheral regions favored the Tai groups that had settled at the margins of these ancient kingdoms. These border populations were able to take advantage of the power vacuum that had been created and founded city-states (*muang*) that for the most part were located to the north, from Burma to Laos, and were the size of small principalities. The lack of a cen-tralized political-administrative structure and the distance from the fertile central plains, which were indispensable for the econ-omy and subsistence of the kingdom, made these *muangs* fragile and unable to expand to control territory beyond the limited confines of their dominion. The situation was destined to change with the development of one of these *muangs* during the reign of the Tai king Indraditya, who was formerly a vassal of the Khmer. In 1238 he succeeded in becoming independent and then set

about securing control of other neighboring cities. This led to the birth of the *muang* of Sukhothai, in the heart of the central plains. That same year witnessed two curious coincidences: the birth, in the north, of the future king of the Tai kingdom of Lan Na, and fur-ther east, of Ngam Muang, who was destined to inherit the king-dom of Phayao, one of the most ancient Tai principalities in the north. At the outset, the 'city-state' of Sukhothai did not attract particular notice, and its history became more animated only with the ascension to the throne of Rama Kamhaeng ('Rama the Bold') in 1275. The kingdom was rather short-lived, lasting for less than two centuries, but had a strong impact. During this period some characteristic features of the cultural history of the future Thailand came to the fore, and above all, a new course in the history of the Tai people began. What made this change so significant was the massive and protracted presence of the Tai in this territory, which was once the heart of the Dvaravati civilization and, more re-cently, of the Khmer sphere of influence. Here the newcomers not only assimilated the Mon traditions, but were somehow also able to master the Khmer political model. When the Tai, who were formerly referred to as 'Siamese' in Cham, Khmer and Burmese writings, founded the *muang* of Sukhothai, the name 'Siam' took on a different meaning, and for the first time defined the people of central Thailand and the territory they inhabited in a political manner. The extension of the kingdom during the reign of Rama Kamhaeng (1275-1298) was a sort of dress rehearsal for what followed almost one hundred years later – the foundation of Ayutthaya, which was much more significant, had a different ideo-logical basis and deeper political-cultural implications. This king achieved unity through alliances with the other Tai rulers of the northern principalities and by means of a series of conquests that

54-55 - The statue of the seated Buddha (Phra Phuttha Chinarat) in Wat Mahathat, Phitsanulok, is one of the most venerated in Thailand.

56 left - A Sukhothai period plate (h. 3 in/8.5 cm) with a painting of a stylized fish (Musée Guimet, Paris).

56 right - This Sukhothai period receptacle is decorated with plant motifs (Rama Kamhaeng National Museum, Sukhothai).

57 - A Yuan dynasty Chinese vase from Wat Phra Pai Luang attests to contact and exchanges between the Sukhothai kingdom and the neighboring countries (Rama Kamhaeng National Museum, Sukhothai).

extended Sukhothai dominion over the central plains and the peninsula of present-day Thailand. Actually, in a similar manner to the rest of South Asia during that time, the direct conquests were limited to the territory surrounding the Tai king's dominion. Once the neighbors had been subjugated by force, there came into play a mechanism of submission that involved not only the new vassals, but their immediate neighbors as well, who thus found themselves in the conquering sovereign's sphere of influence without his having ever occupied their distant lands. So it was that, with the submission of Phetburi, Rama Kamhaeng also obtained the loyalty of the entire peninsula as far as Nakhon Si Thammarat. Two other different initiatives proved to be equally meaningful tools in the move towards cultural cohesion and political unification. The first was the adoption of a writing system – derived from that of the Khmer – for the Thai (or Siamese) language, which was promoted and used by Rama Kamhaeng in the famous inscription of 1292 that celebrates the newly born kingdom and the king's pious government. Already at the end of his reign the inscriptions were carved in Thai, which replaced previous languages. The second, and no less important, measure was the support the royal family gave to Theravada Buddhism. Although it had existed in Thailand for centuries, this was the first time that it became the religion of the people and was the faith sustained and promoted by the kings. An equally beneficial event was the contact established in the mid-13th century between Nakhon Si Thammarat and Sri Lanka, as the Theravadic teachings in the orthodox form established by the Mahavihara of Anuradhapura came from the latter country: from the peninsula to Lan Na and from Sukhothai to Lopburi, this doctrinal renewal and the constant relations with the Singhalese community constituted another major contribu-

tion to the formation of the country's cultural identity. In a self-glorifying inscription of 1292, King Rama Kamhaeng presents himself as the protector of the Dharma and the Buddhist community, always caring for the spiritual well-being of his people, and the creator of the material prosperity of his subjects. During his reign, Buddhism and politics went through a phase of perfect symbiosis that would prove to be one of the components of the formula of government adopted by the rulers of Ayutthaya. From a political standpoint, the kingdom of Sukhothai was a repetition of the ancient power relations that had characterized the distant-past history of Thailand. It was by no means centralized, based on alliances and vassalage and the kingdom of Rama Kamhaeng experienced the cohesive power of the Buddhist faith, in a similar way to the Dvaravati period. This system worked for a while, but did not manage to retain cultural and ethnic unity in a reality that was much more complex than the ancient Mon kingdom. This is likely to be because the Mon community may have been more homogenous ethnically speaking. The ruling family's support of Buddhism continued for the entire Sukhothai period, reaching its peak under Lo Thai and Lu Thai respectively, in the first and second half of the 14th century. However, the reign of these two kings was also marked by the loss of the independence of their *muang*: overwhelmed by the growing power of the neighboring kingdom of Ayutthaya, Sukhothai was first obliged to make a formal act of submission in 1348 and was then annexed by Ayutthaya in 1438. With this passage, the new kingdom demoted the city to the rank of a provincial capital. However, artistic activity continued at least until the 18th century, when the Burmese invasions marked a deathblow for ancient Sukhothai, as well as for Ayutthaya, bringing about their definitive demise.

Before becoming the capital of the kingdom of the same name at the behest of King Rama Kamhaeng in 1278, Sukhothai was an outpost in the remote western Khmer provinces. But there are few traces of this foreign presence in the local architecture and sculpture, as if political independence had followed a period of autonomy marked by a complete break with the past, even in the field of art. This remoteness from Khmer artistic expression is immediately noticeable in the monuments in the ancient capital: a state of detachment can be seen in the different uses made of the edifices, the choice of building materials and architectural decoration, and, above all, the subtle differences that inform the art of this period. The area of the city — now the historic park of Sukhothai — corresponded to a rectangle 5,905 ft by 4,920 ft (1,800 m by 1,500 m), which was surrounded by a triple wall. This consisted of an inner wall made of laterite and a double wall made of beaten earth. Four gates, one on each side, afforded access to the city. This orderly plan, and perhaps the position of the main sanctuary, Wat Mahathat, built in almost the geometric center of the city, have led many scholars to cite a reference to Khmer tradition. However, this seems rather vague here and certainly not as evident in the town planning and architecture as in Ayutthaya. In fact, the city lacks the clear-cut organization in the street network, the precise arrangement of the numerous monuments and the canal and reservoir system that distinguish the structure of the Khmer temple complexes and cities. The ruins lie both inside and outside the ancient boundaries of the city and date to different periods in the short history of this kingdom. The difficulty in establishing exact dates for each period depends above all on the fact that the duration of the kingdom of Sukhothai does not coincide with its artistic development. This is likely to have begun a short time after the foundation of the *muang* and did not end with the annexation to Ayutthaya, but continued until the Burmese invasions in the 18th century, after which the city was abandoned. Furthermore, the custom of building new monuments over the remains of more ancient structures and of renovating the decoration, makes the task of interpretation even more complex. This practice widespread in all Southeast Asia especially as the building materials — such as stucco — proved to be suitable for this type of operation.

58-59 - WAT MAHATHAT IS
THE PRINCIPAL RELIGIOUS
COMPLEX AT SUKHOTHAI AND
LIES IN THE MIDDLE OF THIS
ANCIENT THAI CITY.
THE BUILDINGS DATE FROM
DIFFERENT PERIODS.

59 - IMMEDIATELY NORTH OF
WAT MAHATHAT IS WAT SA SI,
A SANCTUARY WHOSE MOST
CHARACTERISTIC FEATURE IS A
BELL-SHAPED *STUPA* THAT
REMINDS ONE OF THE
ARCHITECTURE IN SRI LANKA.

The most ancient monuments in the Sukhothai area are Wat Phra Phai Luang and Wat Si Sawai; two complexes situated respectively outside and inside the city walls and both dating from the Khmer period. Wat Phra Phai Luang, built during the reign of Jayavarman VII, was a Mahayana temple and was situated north of the city. Originally the complex comprised three sanctuary-towers (*prasat*), to which other structures were added when the temple was converted into a Theravada monastery. Traces of the ancient construction lie in one of the three towers aligned at the end of a *wihan* and made of stuccoed laterite. The heavy structure of the

roof, the absence of movement due to the pilasters on the cella walls, and the building materials used, all hark back to the architecture of Jayavarman VII. However, the precise stucco decoration covering the laterite surfaces was a new innovation: it has nothing in common with the rather crude decoration of the late Khmer monuments and, on the contrary, has the elegance of the ancient Dvaravati tradition. The remains of the *wihan* that precedes the three towers consists of a rectangular brick platform and laterite columns. The elevated brick structure supporting the large *stupa* still has traces of the images of a seated Buddha in the niches and

60-61 - WAT SI SAWAI HAS THREE *PRASATS* THAT WERE BUILT DURING SUKHOTHAI'S ANGKORIAN PERIOD.

61 TOP - THE REMAINS OF A *VIHAN* WITH A BRICK *STUPA* LIE NEXT TO WAT PHRA PAI LUANG *PRASAT*.

61 BOTTOM - ONLY ONE OF THE WAT PHRA PAI LUANG *PRASATS* IS WELL PRESERVED.

of semi-divine figures which, seem to date from the early 15th century. Even more closely bound to its Khmer origin is Wat Si Sawai, bounded by a square enclosure wall that contains three large sanctuary-towers whose foundations date from the Angkorian period. Structures that now appear to be similar to three *prangs* in the Ayutthaya style were probably originally three Khmer *prasats*, which were altered and stuccoed around the second half of the 14th century, the period when the *wihan* was placed in front of the three towers. The only Khmer monument that was not converted into a Buddhist monastery, San Ta Pha Daeng, is a cubic cella made of laterite that was built inside the enclosure wall and can be dated to the first half of the 12th century. In this sanctuary archeologists found some stone statues of Brahmanic divinities, both male and female, which were mounted on circular pedestals and reveal the special care the sculptors took in rendering the jewels and attire. Outside the city wall, a short distance beyond the south gate, lies Wat Kon Laeng, the pyramid-shaped structure built for King Rama Kamhaeng as the seat of Phra Ka-phung, a tutelary spirit of Sukhothai. In the mid-14th century the site was converted to the Buddhist religion.

62 - INSIDE THE ENCLOSURE OF WAT
MAHATHAT AT SUKHOTHAI THERE ARE
VARIOUS COLOSSAL STATUES OF
BUDDHA, SUCH AS THIS ONE THAT
PORTRAYS HIM IN A SEATED POSITION.

62-63 - THE FOCAL POINT OF WAT MAHATHAT IS THE 'LOTUS BUD' *CHEDI* THAT RISES FROM THE PLATFORM IN THE MIDDLE OF THE ENCLOSURE, SURROUNDED BY EIGHT OTHER RELIQUARY TOWERS. TWO SYMMETRICAL *MONDOPS* FLANK THE PLATFORM.

The construction of the great Buddhist monasteries (*wat*) at Sukhothai began in the 14th century and continued for several centuries, even after it was annexed to the kingdom of Ayutthaya. Many old monuments were restored and many new ones added. In a typical configuration, each monastery is surrounded by a rectangular outer wall that contains various edifices. The most important element is the *stupa*, which could be replaced by a *chedi* or *prang*, depending on the period and the site. In any case, the three structures have features in common: they are all reliquaries and they attract the attention of the faithful because of their central position inside the enclosure, they have considerable height (as they always stand on elevated platforms) and they are articulated with many molded elements. The three terms are used here to underscore the differences between the types of commemorative monuments, which for the most part concern the shape of the 'body' of each one. Whereas the *stupa* may be either hemispheric or bell-shaped, and the entire monument has a symbolism and a configuration (base, body, pinnacle, etc.) that is clearly distinguishable. There is a great variety of types of *chedi*, in which the shape of body is not as important, it may be a 'lotus bud,' bell-shaped, cubic and so on, because of the development of the base and the upward thrust of the monument roof. After the *stupa*, the most important edifices in the monastery are the *bot* and the *wihan*. The term *bot* is an abbreviation of *ubosot* (*uposathaghara* in the Pali language) and is a rectangular hall much like a *wihan*, or prayer hall. It is mainly used for the ordination of the monks. As a sign of the importance of the *bot* — the only room inside the *wat*, which, however, has more than one *wihan* — eight 'boundary stones' (*sima*) mark off the edifice area. These leaf-shaped stone steles are placed in correspondence with the four cardinal points and the four intermediate points along the perimeter of the building, precisely above the place where, on the occasion of the inauguration of the *bot*, the 'stone spheres' or *luk nimit* are buried. This latter ceremony marks the consecration of the ground on which the religious edifice stands. For this reason,

nine stones are placed in correspondence with the four cardinal points, the four intermediate ones, and the middle point. This is where the statue of Buddha is placed inside the *bot*. The *wihan* – taken from the Sanskrit word *vihara*, which was originally used to indicate a residence of the monastic community – is an assembly hall that is rectangular and opens eastward. This is where the lay community gathers for special ceremonies and where the most precious images of Buddha contained in the *wat* are placed. Inside the enclosure, there may also be open pavilions (*sala*) that are used as resting places or for lay activities. There are also the *prasada*, a build-

prayers and for the shared celebrations of both the monks and lay community. While the alignment of the *chedi* and *wihan* on the East-West axis appears to have been a constant feature in the monasteries built in this period, the placement of the other elements in the monastic structure was left more to the discretion of the builders. However, there was a tendency toward a symmetrical arrangement around the main axis. An example of this is the *bot*, which in the architecture of Ayutthaya usually faced the *wihan*, while at Sukhothai it was generally parallel to the *chedi* platform. Another common feature of Sukhothai architecture are the *mondops*, which look

ing used by the royal family and the *mondop*, a closed and square pavilion. This has a roof constructed with superposed, inclined cornices that was used to house a precious object, an image of Buddha or especially valuable sacred texts. During the Sukhothai period, the *stupa* or reliquary tower (*chedi*) stood in the middle of a square or rectangular area that was generally delimited by a simple enclosure wall with entrances in one or more points. Near this tower, and also aligned on the main East-West axis, was the *wihan*, the rectangular columned hall. Originally this building had a tiled wooden roof, along the thick back wall of which there might have been a stuccoed brick statue of Buddha. The *wihan* was used for

like large, square brick buildings with a single slit-like opening to the east. The *mondops* have thick walls and as no roofs exist now, we can only surmise about their appearance. It is thought that they could have been overhanging as the reduced size of the structure allowed for this, or made of wood coated with stucco. The *mondops* were decorated on the outside with stucco compositions that covered the walls depicting episodes from the life of the Enlightened One. Within the interior, they contained colossal statues of Buddha – the so-called *phra attharot*, an expression indicating an image of Buddha about 28 ft. (8.5 m) tall. The buildings have a rectangular plan and rather thick walls that conceal the impressive statue,

64 - THE MAIN *CHEDI* AT WAT MAHATHAT IS CROWNED BY A TAPERING SPIRE. THE TEMPLE, FOUNDED BY KING RAMA KAMHAENG, WAS THE RELIGIOUS FULCRUM OF SUKHOTHAI.

65 TOP LEFT - A VIEW OF WAT MAHATHAT SHOWING TWO OF ITS *STUPAS*.

65 TOP RIGHT - REMAINS OF OTHER *STUPAS* LIE ALONG THE SOUTH SIDE OF THE WAT MAHATHAT ENCLOSURE.

65 BOTTOM - ON THE MAIN AXIS OF WAT MAHATHAT, BETWEEN THE COLUMNS OF THE *WIHAN*, IS A COLOSSAL STATUE OF THE SEATED BUDDHA.

which can be seen only from the opening on the east side. The rest of the space in the interior of the monastery walls was occupied by additional *wihans*, *chedis* and *stupas* that were small and arranged in an orderly manner on either side of the East-West axis, or scattered within the enclosure. The Temple of the Great Relic, or Wat Mahathat, is a particularly well-developed complex, with over 200 *chedis* and numerous *wihans* and *mondops*. It was founded by King Rama Kamhaeng at the end of the 13th century and enlarged by his son Lothai in the first half of the 14th century. This monastery, like all royal foundations, was not used to house a community of resident monks, but still has the principal features of Thai Buddhist complexes. Furthermore, since it has received many donations over the centuries, it contains what is in effect, a collection of various types of reliquary tower. The original nucleus of Wat Mahathat is the *chedi* that lies on a platform in the middle of the enclosure. Hidden inside the *chedi* is the pyramid-shaped base on which Rama Kamhaeng received the oath of allegiance from his allies. In the first decades of the 14th century, a monument containing a relic of Buddha was built at the same point, and in 1340 two other relics were added, taken there by the monk-prince Si Satha upon his return from a journey to Sri Lanka. One of these is a *chedi* in the shape of a 'lotus bud,' the type of reliquary tower elaborated at Sukhothai at the beginning of the 14th century. The structure consists of a tall, square platform surmounted by a tripartite, notched base, which in turn is topped by a tall socle that supports the 'lotus bud' of the *chedi*. The monument is crowned with a tapered spire. On the same platform, around the *chedi*, there are eight reliquary towers

in different styles. The four at the cardinal points are made of laterite and have a shape that resembles a Khmer *prasat*, and the four corner ones are made of bricks and imitate the type of *stupa-prasat* that originated with Srivijaya art and then spread throughout Thailand. All around the base of the main platform is a stucco frieze depicting a procession of monks with folded hands carrying out the circumambulation ritual (*pradaksina*) around the monument. This type of decoration seems to be an exception compared to the more common platform decorations of images of elephants made of stuccoed brick that are repeatedly found in other monuments. Inside the *wat* enclosure there is a great variety of *chedis* and *stupas*, which almost constitute a sample of the all of the forms that were common in the Sukhothai period and beyond. Among these is the so-called *ratna-cetiya* ('jewel-*stupa*'), which imitates a prototype from Haripunchai, the Mon kingdom that flourished in northern Thailand from the 8th to the 13th century. This type consists of a multi-story pyramid, each level of which has three niches on each side containing statues of a standing Buddha. Another type of *chedi* is also evident, deriving from the 13th-century Wat Kukut of Lamphun, this *chedi* was built during the 14th and 15th centuries. Of more uncertain derivation, but again built with a pyramid shape on a square plan, are the remains of a large *stupa* situated south of Wat Mahathat *chedi*. These two monuments are the largest in the monastery. On the north and south sides of the central platform of Wat Mahathat are two brick *mondops*, each of which houses a *phra attharot*. Lastly, the remains of a *bot* and a *wihan* can be seen in the sectors to the north and east of the court, respectively.

66 - THE TWO SMALL RELIQUARY TOWERS ON WAT MAHATHAT'S CENTRAL PLATFORM WERE CLEARLY INFLUENCED BY KHMER ARCHITECTURE (LEFT) AND THE ART OF SRIVIJAYA (RIGHT).

67 - THIS PERFECTLY PRESERVED STATUE OF THE SEATED BUDDHA STANDS AT THE FOOT OF A LARGE PYRAMID-SHAPED *STUPA* IN WAT MAHATHAT.

**68** LEFT - THE WALLS OF THE BUILDINGS IN THE WAT MAHATHAT COMPLEX HAVE FINE STUCCO DECORATION, SUCH AS THIS REPRESENTATION OF THE BIRTH OF BUDDHA.

**68-69** - AROUND THE CENTRAL PLATFORM OF WAT MAHATHAT ARE BUILDINGS AND STRUCTURES WITH DIFFERENT ARCHITECTURAL FORMS.

**69** TOP - THE COLUMNS OF THE PRINCIPAL *WIHAN* OF WAT MAHATHAT DIRECT OUR GAZE TO THE STATUE OF THE SEATED BUDDHA, SEEN HERE FROM THE BACK.

**69** BOTTOM - THIS DETAIL OF THE STUCCO FRIEZE THAT DECORATES THE BASE OF THE CENTRAL PLATFORM OF WAT MAHATHAT SHOWS A PROCESSION OF MONKS WALKING AROUND THE MONUMENT.

Inside the ancient city walls, west of Wat Mahathat, lies Wat Trapang Ngoen, a monastery constructed in the late 14th century set in the middle of an artificial lake. This complex comprises a small *bot*, a *wihan* and a 'lotus bud' *chedi*. The special relationship with Sri Lanka also explains certain architectural and decorative borrowings. It was the cradle of the Theravada Buddhist tradition, to which the kingdom of Sukhothai turned during the reign of King Lu Thai in order to assimilate the teachings and organize the Buddhist community. A case in point is the campaniform, stucco-coated brick *stupa* of Wat Chang Lom (late 14th century) and its platform, which is supported by a group of elephants whose bodies protrude from the niches. Although it derives from Sri Lankan art, the elephant-atlas style, the model of the *stupa* has been interpreted here in an original manner. This can most obviously be seen in the platform, be it square or round, which is always elevated and may have superposed steps.

Another fine example is Wat Sa Si, which lies a short distance from Wat Mahathat in the middle of an artificial lake; its campaniform *stupa*, made of bricks and in the Singhalese style, is preceded by a *wihan* and flanked by a *stupa-prasat*. Wat Chedi Si Hong (early 15th century) lies outside the wall, south of the city and has a bell-shaped *stupa* built on a platform decorated with a series of stucco elephants that alternate with figures of semi-divine beings. Despite the rather poor state of preservation, the high quality of the elegant relief can still be clearly seen. Lastly, situated respectively west and south of the city, are the Wat Saphan Hin and Wat Chetupon monasteries. The former, standing on the top of a hill a few kilometers from Sukhothai, houses the ruins of a *wihan* and a colossal statue (*phra attharot*) of the standing Buddha. The latter monastery, on the other hand, consists of the remains of various brick and laterite structures, which contain two large images of Buddha, one standing and the other walking.

70 TOP LEFT - THE COLOSSAL STATUE OF A STANDING BUDDHA TOWERS OVER THE RUINS OF WAT SAPHAN HIN MONASTERY, WHICH WAS CONSTRUCTED ON A HILL NEAR SUKHOTHAI.

70 TOP RIGHT - AT THE FOOT OF THE 'LOTUS BUD' SPIRE OF WAT TRAPANG NGOEN IS A STATUE OF THE SEATED BUDDHA.

70 BOTTOM - WAT CHETUPON MONASTERY, LYING AMONG THE RUINS OF A *MONDOP* PAVILION, HAS A STATUE OF BUDDHA WALKING.

71 - WAT SA SI IS SITUATED NEAR WAT MAHATHAT, IN THE MIDDLE OF AN ARTIFICIAL LAKE. NEXT TO THE BELL-SHAPED *STUPA* (RIGHT) IS A *STUPA-PRASAT*.

72 AND 73 TOP -
ELEPHANTS MADE OF
STUCCOED BRICK SEEM
TO EMERGE FROM THE
NICHES IN THE SQUARE
PLATFORM THAT SUPPORTS
WAT CHANG LOM'S *STUPA*
AT SUKHOTHAI.

73 BOTTOM - AT SI SATCHANALAI
IS WAT CHANG LOM, A BUILDING
SHARING SOME SIMILARITIES WITH
THE IMPRESSIVE MONUMENT AT
SUKHOTHAI. THE CAMPANIFORM
*STUPA* STANDS ON A TALL BASE
DECORATED WITH FIGURES OF
ELEPHANTS.

# SUKHOTHAI SCULPTURE

It was precisely in this period that new aesthetic research commenced, the best results of which are undoubtedly the superb 14th- and 15th-century representations of Buddha, which are arguably the most original expression of all Thai art. For the first time, Buddha is depicted in all four positions described in the texts: seated in the *virasana* and *bhumisparsamudra* positions, walking or standing – especially with his right hand making the *vitarkamudra* gesture – and lying on his right side. More than any other, the image created by Sukhothai artists represents the felicitous attempt to translate within the limits of an artificial form, Buddha as a *mahapurusa*, or 'superior being.' Thus, he is distinguished by the perfect attributes he acquired during his innumerable existences. Hence the sculptors' invention of a formal vocabulary capable of alluding to the supernatural essence of the Enlightened One. In this way they were able to describe their ability in evoking spiritual perfection through the signs, gestures, proportions and dimensions of a transfigured human body. In fact, otherworldly reality is revealed not in the anatomical truth or realism of the body, the perfection of the various components or the balanced proportions – all signs, once again, of human excellence – but appears in a mysterious and inscrutable manner in the surreal forms to which the human body has been transformed. The Sukhothai school represents Buddha with the greatest number of distinguishing features (*laksana*) ever detailed. Conventionally, Buddha's body has 32 principal 'signs' (*laksana*) and 80 secondary ones, that are distinctive of a 'great being' (*mahapurusa*). Besides the most important ones, the *urna* and the *usnisa*, that is, the two protuberances situated respectively between the eyebrows and on the top of his head, Buddha's other distinguishing signs include the palms of his hands and the soles of his feet marked by a wheel (*cakra*), his powerful chest, wide shoulders, tapering fingers, melodious voice, white teeth, long eyebrows, wide forehead, golden complexion and prominent nose. Of all these signs, only a few are depicted by the sculpture schools of Buddhist Asia, while others were either ignored or were rendered in a particular manner. In Thailand, it was the Sukhothai artists who showed great interest in this figurative code and attempted to represent the greatest number of *laksana*. Some of them faithfully mirror the poetic descriptions in

the non-canonical texts. Some of these examples describe his arms as looking like an 'elephant's trunk,' his nose curved like 'a parrot's beak,' his legs similar 'to those of an antelope,' his 'protruding' heels, his chin shaped like 'a mango' and his fingers like 'young lotus buds.' To these signs was added the 'trademark' of Sukhothai art, which was utilized by all the later sculpture schools: the flame that rises from the *usnisa* and, according to Buddhist texts, represents the enrichment of supreme consciousness and knowledge. Depicted in the shape of a flame by the Sukhothai artists in order to allude to the luminosity emanating from the figure of Buddha, and in the form of a jewel much like a lotus bud by other schools, to underscore its ornamental nature, this sign (never so evident as in Sukhothai art) originated in India in the sphere of two different sculptural traditions that were widespread in Southeast Asia. In keeping with Indian tradition, these images are not rendered realistically but rather celebrate the state of harmony and peace attained by the Enlightened One. Therefore, no bulging muscle, angular bone or joint, or pulsating vein can alter the state of perfect poise and peace of mind so aptly expressed by the curved and uninterrupted forms of Buddha's body. The essence of the Sukhothai style, leaving aside the ingenious iconography and the technical perfection of the newly created images, would seem to be epitomized in the repetition of the curved line, which is indeed taken to extremes. The result is pertinent already in the seated statues, where the arch of his oval face is mirrored in his eyebrows, in his almond-shaped eyes and chin. An undulating rhythm can be seen radiating from his face to his chest and from his rounded shoulders to the arch created by his crossed legs. This manifestation is even more surprising in the image of the walking Buddha. This creation, for which the Sukhothai school of sculpture is world-famous – for having invented the free-standing icon of the walking Buddha – dates from the late-13th century or the beginning of the 14th century. Surreal in its movement toward liberation and nothingness, this portrait of Buddha is a triumph of technical perfection and attention to detail: the right leg slightly bent, in a weightless, airy movement; the right arm loose and as supple as a liana; the left hand in the *vitarkamudra* position and the perfect oval of the face, which is noble and relaxed.

75 - A DETAIL OF A HAND OF THE COLOSSAL STATUE OF BUDDHA MADE OF BRICKS CASED WITH STUCCO LOCATED IN THE WAT SI CHUM COMPLEX AT SUKHOTHAI.

The production of images inspired by the 'classical' Sukhothai style continued even after the end of the independence of the *muang*, but the formula of the former masterpieces was abandoned. The former intensity and spirituality was dampened somewhat by the rather mannered repetition, and iconographic orthodoxy was responsible for certain alterations. These can bee seen in the representation of the fingers, now with equal length, as can be seen in one of the most popular images in Thailand, the statue in gilded bronze of the seated Buddha (Phra Phuttha Chinarat) in Wat Mahathat at Phitsanulok. The influence of Sukhothai is also reflected in the sculpture that shows Brahmanic inspiration produced between the 14th and 16th centuries. An example of this art is a group of bronze statues, most of which are very large, depicting some of the Hindu gods; Shiva, Vishnu and Brahma in a style that has much in common with that of Buddhist sculpture. The group includes some more ancient statues found at Sukhothai and more recent ones from Kamphaeng Phet. All of these works are solemn and a bit austere, decorated with very sophisticated jewels which, together with the attire, betray the difference between the two groups. However, the Sukhothai statues seem to be more receptive to the inspiration of Sri Lanka, while those of Kamphaeng Phet, which were executed at a later stage, evoke Khmer motifs that probably came by way of Ayutthaya.

76 - THIS STATUE OF THE SEATED BUDDHA IN THE *BHUMISPARSAMUDRA* POSITION (H. 26.7 IN/68 CM), A FINE EXAMPLE OF SUKHOTHAI ART, STILL BEARS TRACES OF ITS ORIGINAL RED LACQUER AND GILDING (NATIONAL MUSEUM, BANGKOK).

77 - THIS GILDED BRONZE STATUE REPRESENTS HARIHARA, A FIGURE COMBINING VISHNU AND SHIVA, AND BELONGS TO A SERIES OF STATUES OF BRAHMAN DIVINITIES EXECUTED DURING THE SUKHOTHAI PERIOD (NATIONAL MUSEUM, BANGKOK).

78 LEFT - THE MASTERFUL SKILL OF THE SUKHOTHAI SCULPTORS IS EXEMPLIFIED IN THIS BRONZE STATUE OF THE WALKING BUDDHA (H. 7 FT 2 IN/220 CM). THE SINUOUS POSTURE OF THE BODY IS MIRRORED IN THE FOLDS OF THE MANTLE (NATIONAL MUSEUM, BANGKOK).

78 RIGHT - THIS HAND OF A BRONZE STATUE OF BUDDHA IS IN THE *VITARKAMUDRA* POSITION (NATIONAL MUSEUM, PHNOM PENH).

79 - THIS BRONZE HEAD OF BUDDHA (H. 2 FT 5 IN/76 CM) FROM KAMPHAENG PHET WAS SCULPTED IN THE FINAL PERIOD OF THE ARTISTIC PRODUCTION OF SUKHOTHAI (NATIONAL MUSEUM, BANGKOK).

# BUDDHA, THE GODS AND THE GENII OF THE LAND

Present-day Thailand is a country with a Theravada Buddhist tradition, which represents one of the ancient schools of Indian Buddhism that rose up after the death of Buddha. According to tradition, around the mid-3rd century BC Theravada Buddhism spread in South India and Sri Lanka. There the Mahavihara, the 'great monastery,' was built, the Pali canon was set down in writing in the 1st century BC and, after various struggles with other Buddhist currents, the Mahavihara community became the sole representative of Theravada orthodoxy. It was from Sri Lanka, or perhaps from Burma, that missionaries set out for Thailand and propagated their doctrine among the Mon population of Dvaravati. The contemporaneous presence of Mahayana Buddhism, in a form that varied in both tone and practice, as well as that of Vajrayana Buddhism, which mostly spread during the Khmer dominion, contributed to making Thai Buddhism particularly syncretic and receptive to other religious practices in the country. Signs of this tendency have been noted already in Mahayana Buddhism filled with Hindu concepts that was observed by Khmer rulers. Traces remained in the idea of a sacred monarchy and in many court rituals, some of which were celebrated up to the ear-

ly 20th century, it is a combination of Hindu and Buddhist rites that can only be separated and distinguished with difficulty. The high point in the process of synthesis among the various traditions was attained in the Sukhothai period, when the Buddhist doctrine was officially accepted by King Rama Kamhaeng, who set about zealously propagating it. One of his grandchildren, King Lu Thai (1347-1368 ca.), gave further impulse to the doctrine by inviting some Singhalese monks to establish the rules of monastic ordination and organize the Buddhist 'church' in keeping with the Mahavihara tradition of Sri Lanka. This latter ruler is also attributed with writing the *Traiphum* (The Three Worlds), a sort of summary of Buddhist cosmological and eschatological concepts complemented by tales and legends from both Indian and local traditions. The consolidation of the Buddhist tradition and its accommodation of ideas inherited from the past and from local traditions, continued in the following centuries. During the period of Ayutthaya, various rulers devoted their energies to preserving Theravada orthodoxy, so much so that during the reign of the pious Dhammaraja II, in the first half of the 18th century, the Thai *sangha* was a model for the Singhalese community.

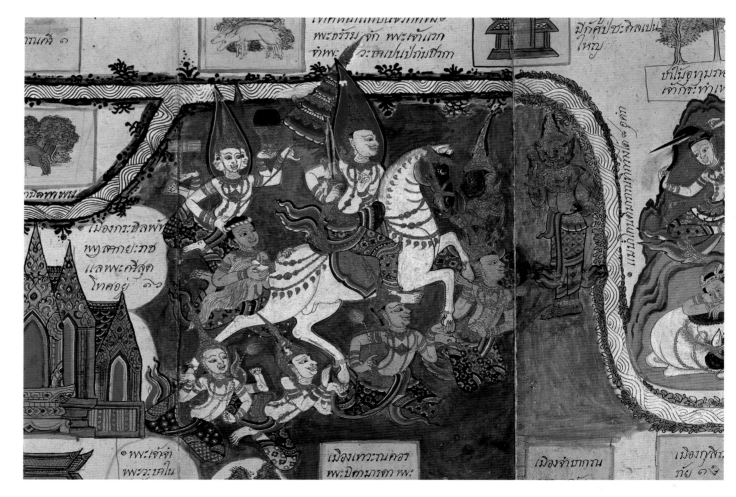

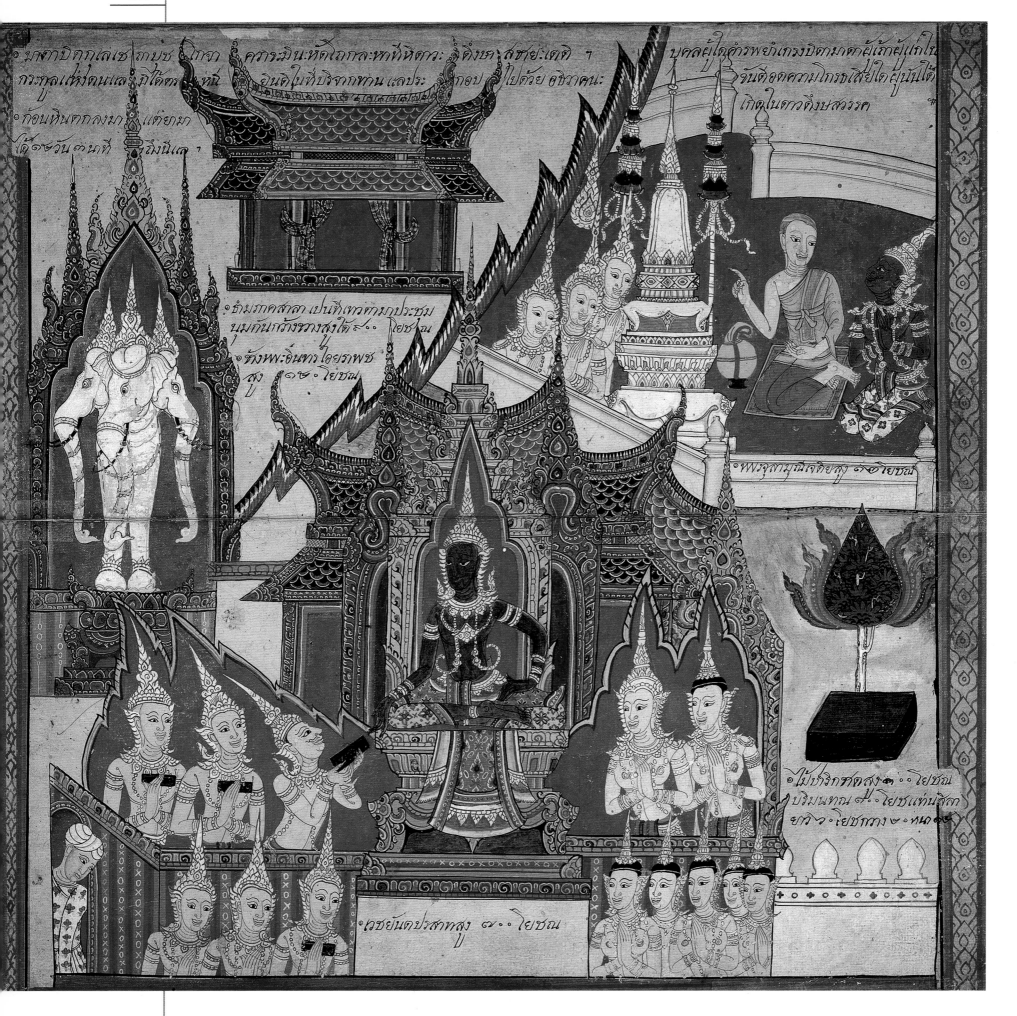

Three monks were sent from Sri Lanka to Ayutthaya to be ordained, and a group of Thai monks went to Sri Lanka, where they stayed for several years. Lastly, other religious reforms took place during the reign of Mongkut (1851-1868), who had been a monk for almost thirty years before ascending the throne and who carried out a program of reform to monastic life based on rigid discipline. The world vision that unites Buddha and the genii of the land, human beings and the gods in a coherent and operative system, is the one evoked by the *Traiphum*, a treatise on cosmology attributed to King Lu Thai, various illustrated manuscripts of which still exist. The three worlds mentioned in the title correspond to the division of the universe, derived from Indian cosmology, into a 'world of desire' (*kamaloka*), a 'world of form' (*rupaloka*), and a 'world without form' (*arupaloka*). Like one of the huge frescoes that decorate the interior of the Thai *bots*, all the forms of visible and invisible existence are included in the description of the *kamaloka*. This consists of the tripartite space of the earth, the underworld and the sky, populated by the Brahmanic gods and by a multitude of supernatural beings that interact with the world of humans, in keeping with a vision common to diverse South Asian cultures. At first sight the idea of a pantheon might appear alien to Theravada Buddhism which, though in theory it does not deny the existence of a supernatural world, in reality it keeps the latter in the background, and concentrates on spiritual progress achieved by means of rigorous discipline. This concession to the domain of the spiritual reveals the emergence of the indigenous religious substratum and its assimilation into the official religion and, vice versa, the accommodation of Buddhist thought to the needs and sensibility of the local culture. The entire structure revolves around the mythical Mount Meru; the center of the universe, surrounded by seven concentric mountain chains and separated by seven seas. All around them, the primordial oceans are said to lap against four island-continents. The southernmost one, known as Jambudvipa (the 'Rose Apple Island'), is the realm of human beings. Between the base of the mountain submerged in the ocean waters and the peak that touches the heavens there are various levels, which house, from the caves in the base upwards, the *asura* (demons), *naga* (serpents who guard the treasures) and other chthonic and ethereal semi-divinities. In the underground regions, there is the underworld itself, divided into four warm and four cold sections. The gods live on the top of the mountain, in the palace whose lord is the god Indra. The infernal abyss and heavenly beatitudes epitomize the opposing conditions that every human being may experience when he/she is reborn. According to the principle of karma retribution, the acts of a person during his existence may lead to six different possible rebirths: condemned to the underworld, as an animal, a tormented soul (or 'famished spirit'), a demon, a god (*deva*) or a human. Although certain states (that of the human and *deva*) are more desirable than others, all six entail remaining in the state of *samsara*, the transcendence of which is the final objective of one's religious quest. In this perspective, the blessed existence of the heavenly gods is superior to that of human beings (the gods are more beautiful, radiant and live for longer) but equally ephemeral. In the celestial space above Mt. Meru are the levels of the *rupaloka* and *arupaloka*; worlds of spiritual perfection populated by divine beings of a superior status that are divided into various classes.

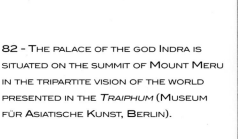

82 - THE PALACE OF THE GOD INDRA IS SITUATED ON THE SUMMIT OF MOUNT MERU IN THE TRIPARTITE VISION OF THE WORLD PRESENTED IN THE *TRAIPHUM* (MUSEUM FÜR ASIATISCHE KUNST, BERLIN).

83 TOP - SUPERNATURAL BEINGS ANIMATE THE SCENES ILLUSTRATING THIS EDITION OF THE *TRAIPHUM* (MUSEUM FÜR ASIATISCHE KUNST, BERLIN).

83 BOTTOM - A SCENE DEPICTING THE BIRTH OF SIDDHARTHA DECORATES A PAGE IN THE *TRAIPHUM*, THE THEOLOGICAL SUMMA OF THAI BUDDHISM. THIS PAGE IS PART OF A MANUSCRIPT THAT ACCORDING TO TRADITION WAS COMMISSIONED BY KING TAKSIN IN 1776 (MUSEUM FÜR ASIATISCHE KUNST, BERLIN).

However, this sophisticated transcendental concept is considered secondary in both artistic depictions and literary descriptions compared to the interest aroused by the *kamaloka*. This is the domain of human vicissitudes, in which each individual can seek his/her own path from the *samsara* cycle. It is an endless journey that binds humans, existence after existence, to painful impermanence, the final journey being an ascension to a higher level of consciousness: total liberation (*nirvana*). But with respect to this goal, which is distant for a monk and extremely remote for a lay person, religion is called upon to respond, and to a certain degree adjust, to other more urgent and human needs. Therefore, the quest for freedom from the chain of rebirths is replaced by the more modest hope of a felicitous rebirth. In order to achieve this state one must carry out meritorious acts in keeping with canonical doctrine, while at the same time not rejecting propitiatory practices that help to avoid the torments of the underworld. And it is precisely in the world of superstition and magic rituals that the 'popular' religious feeling that characterizes most Thai Buddhist practices comes to the fore so forcefully. An example of this coexistence is the veneration of the footprints of Buddha (*buddhapada*) that is housed in various small temples scattered throughout the country. Paying homage to the holy footprints is considered an act that helps one avert the risk of ending up in hell. The requests made to Buddhist monks for prophesy, amulets and formulas against illness and misfortune belong to the same line of thought.

84-85 - THIS SLAB OF CARVED STONE (H. 11 IN/28 CM) BELONGS TO THE SERIES OF SCENES PLACED ALONG THE HIDDEN CORRIDOR OF THE *MONDOP* OF WAT SI CHUM AT SUKHOTHAI.

THE SCENE DEPICTS AN EPISODE FROM THE *JATAKA*, THE STORIES OF THE PREVIOUS LIVES OF BUDDHA, IN A VIVIDLY PICTORIAL MANNER (NATIONAL MUSEUM, BANGKOK).

An important role in the religious life of Thailand is played by the belief in the *phi*, supernatural beings who act as genii of the land and live in every part of the country. Gifted with power superior to that of humans and with an ambiguous nature that can transform them into either benevolent or evil beings, depending on the circumstances, the *phi* govern many aspects of daily life. They are constantly beseeched to protect humans from danger as well as to guarantee good luck, well-being and prosperity. For this reason they have homage and gifts bestowed upon them. They are believed to use their power mainly on the earth, and this sharing of the same space with humans assures that the supernatural is constantly present in everyday life, as if it were a world parallel to the human dimension. Mountains, lakes, rivers and forests are populated by invisible spirits that Thai Buddhism has incorporated into its ceremonies, explained in its own legends, and has systematically placed in the cosmological vision of the *Traiphum*. In order to gain the favor of a *phi*, one offers him an 'abode' or 'base': an altar built inside one's house or in a temple serves to protect its inhabitants and acknowledges the sovereignty of the local genie over that space. There are a great many *phi* and they are all of different origin: genii of the land, spirits of ancestors, spirits of people who died a violent death, and divinities in the Indian Brahmanic pantheon (for example, Indra) that have been elevated to the status of tutelary genii. By means of a process of assimilation, whose procedures are well known in Mahayana, Thai Buddhism incorporated into its system a multitude of supernatural powers whose numbers continue to increase to this day. The basis of this coexistence is rooted in the distant past, as can be seen by a passage from the famous inscription of King Rama Kamhaeng. He was the ruler of Sukhothai who, in establishing Buddhism as the state religion, invited his subjects to honor the tutelary genie of the *muang*

(Phra Kaphung) to guarantee the security and prosperity of the kingdom. The cult of the *phis*, especially that of the tutelary genie of the region, therefore also contains the ancient ancestral tradition, common to the culture of South Asia, of the 'spirit of the mountain.' This spirit was once venerated through the construction of *menhirs* and, in more recent times, in the pillars placed in the middle of the villages (*lak ban*) or cities (*lak muang*). Like the mountain, of which it is a replacement, this symbol is a sort of bridge between the world of the living and the world of the dead. It serves to link the two levels and allows for the transfer of the charismatic power of an ancestor or the power of the local genie to the village chief. It also aids in promoting equilibrium between the world of humans and that of the spirits. Testimony of this sensibility can be found throughout the history of Thailand: the persistence of the cult of the god of the land can be noted in the artificial pyramids built outside the city walls from the Sukhothai period up to the kingdom of Bangkok. An example is the four-terrace structure of Wat Kon Laeng, built in the 13th century at Sukhothai, the Phu Khao Thong of Ayutthaya, and also the so-called Gold Mountain in Bangkok. Within the latter, the ancient animistic tradition of the spirit of the mountain is merged with the most recent of Buddhist traditions. And it is difficult not to recognize the archetype of the mountain even in the forms of the *stupas*, *chedis* and *prangs*, whose profile is a clear reference to Mt. Meru, the mythical cosmic mountain in the middle of the universe, the hub around which the world is organized. Therefore, in the presentation of a temple or sanctuary, one can note the various layers that, over the centuries, have given rise to religious syncretism. Within in this system, the teachings of Buddha live side by side – without the slightest contradiction – with local beliefs and practices regarding the relations between Man and the supernatural.

86 AND 87 - THE TEMPLE OF THE GOLD MOUNTAIN IN BANGKOK STANDS OUT AGAINST THE ANCIENT HEART OF THE CITY AND IS THE HOME OF THE TUTELARY GENIUS OF THIS SITE.

THIS STRUCTURE, IN WHICH THE MOUNTAIN AND THE *STUPA* ARE MERGED, REPRESENTS THE SYNTHESIS OF THE ANCIENT LOCAL CULT AND BUDDHIST DOCTRINE.

Henri Mouhot, the French naturalist who traveled throughout Indochina in 1858, wrote that at Ayutthaya "the only relics of the ancient city are the myriad *wats*, or temples, most of which are in ruins. They occupy an area of several miles and are hidden by the plants that have grown around them." And indeed, very little could be seen at that time of the ancient splendor of the 'invincible capital' – the meaning of Ayutthaya, a Thai transliteration of 'Ayodhya,' the birthplace of the hero of the *Ramayana* – after the 1767 sacking by the Burmese. They had partly or totally damaged many large religious complexes and had ruined the much more perishable wooden civil architecture. The *muang* was founded in 1350 by Prince U Thong, after he had arrived from the province of Suphanburi, and represented the unification of the country for over 400 years. By the time he was crowned king in 1351 with the throne name of Ramathibodi, U Thong had already taken control of the territory of Lopburi and secured the submission of the Tai kingdom of Sukhothai. Under these circumstances, Ayutthaya aimed to write the last chapter in the history of the ancient kingdoms of Southeast Asia, which had included Pagan and Angkor. The ambitious plan to emulate the glorious past took shape in less than a century thanks to the rulers' capacity in assimilating the heritage of the kingdoms of Sukhothai and Lopburi. Features of both were amalgamated into the new kingdom, which for the first time took on a cultural and political reality that was not only Tai. The assimilation of the administrative-bureaucratic apparatus and of the Khmer concept of royalty, together with the innovative creation of a hierarchical social structure and the organization of manpower, were the basic elements in the growth and rise of the new kingdom. The first half of the 15th century saw the successful domination of the region from Sukhothai to Songkhla.

88 - A BRONZE ELEMENT ON A CHARIOT DEPICTING GARUDA GRASPING THE *NAGAS* (NATIONAL MUSEUM, BANGKOK).

89 - THE ARTISTIC ACTIVITY AT AYUTTHAYA IS REPRESENTED BY THE 'U THONG STYLE,' AN EXAMPLE OF WHICH IS THIS BRONZE STATUE OF THE SEATED BUDDHA (H. 27 IN/70 CM; CHAO SAM PHRAYA NATIONAL MUSEUM, AYUTTHAYA).

Situated in the middle of the central plains, Ayutthaya was in an ideal position: it had the natural defense of the waterway surrounding it, and that same water also provided it with a natural commercial outlet. Taking advantage of the political stability it had achieved, the kingdom expanded, first eastward with the conquest of Angkor and then northward with the capture of Sukhothai, However, Lan Na remained unconquered. But its true wealth came from international commerce, which transformed the city into a major trading station between the East and West. Since the capital was easy to reach by sea via the Chao Phraya River, its economic fortune was predominantly connected to trade with the Chinese Empire, to which Ayutthaya regularly sent tributes. Trade increased with the arrival of Islamic merchants from India and Persia. The economic prosperity and cosmopolitan atmosphere of the city soon attracted Westerners as well. First came the Portuguese in the early 16th century, followed by

the Spanish and, in the 17th century, the Dutch, English and French. It was the Dutch who mainly took advantage of the opportunity for prosperous and lasting business. Trade was based on the exportation of deer hides to Japan, and the monopoly was granted to the Dutch by the Thai rulers. Further trade included the exportation of rice to nearby Batavia (now North Jakarta) and the importation of luxury items from the Western world. In the cultural synthesis that occurred during this period, the various components that merged with the legacy of Ayutthaya assumed the form of a theocratic concept of royalty. According to this, the king had a divine nature and, from the time he ascended the throne, was identified with one of the superior Brahmanic gods. He was celebrated with rituals and gifts, the repositories of which were the court Brahmans. At the same time, however, the king was presented to his subjects as a Dharmaraja, a 'king (protector) of Buddhist Law.'

90 - THE USE OF BLACK LACQUER
AND GILDING DEVELOPED DURING
THE AYUTTHAYA PERIOD AND REACHED
ITS HEIGHT WITH THE ARTISTIC PRODUCTION
OF BANGKOK (NATIONAL MUSEUM,
BANGKOK).

91 - THE MOST HIGHLY PRIZED EXAMPLES
OF LACQUERED AND GILDED CHESTS, SUCH
AS THIS ONE, WERE MADE FOR THE ROYAL
COURT OR THE MONASTERIES, WHERE THEY
WERE USED TO CONTAIN MANUSCRIPTS
(MUSÉE GUIMET, PARIS).

Thus, while the kings' court manner and their conduct with respect to their subjects and the Buddhist community were based on the teachings of the Enlightened One, as had been the case with the kings of Sukhothai, the nature of royalty, the complex royal ceremony and the administration of the state were codified by the rituals and protected by the gods of Hinduism, all elements that derived from the Khmer civilization. After passing through a critical and ravaging period of wars with the neighboring populations in the second half of the 16th century, Ayutthaya enjoyed a period of splendor and prosperity that lasted for the entire 17th century. The symbol of this period of wealth and security is Wat Chaiwatthanaram, the monument that was revived in a Buddhist manner, highlighting the idea, which harks back to the Angkor period in Cambodia, of the orderly universe whose terrestrial tutelary was the king himself. Other artistic production in this period reveals the importance attached to the idea of royalty and its association with Buddhism: the most interesting instances of this are the numerous statues of the Enlightened One standing, adorned with royal insignia, which had already been produced in the 12th to 13th centuries and again became fashionable from the 16th century on. According to one possible interpretation, the iconography of the image of the adorned Buddha is related to the legend of King Jambupati, the haughty monarch who was overwhelmed by the words and humility of Buddha, who appeared to him in the magnificent guise of a universal sovereign. The sumptuous bronze sculptures depicting the Hindu divinities must be included in the same context of the celebration of royalty. While the official religion continued to be Buddhism, the main gods of Hinduism became the archetypes of royalty for the Siamese monarchs and, likewise, the 'indifference' shown by Buddhist culture regarding worldly affairs was compensated by the culture of the court Brahmans. They were experts in astrology and the administration of the kingdom, as well as in ceremonial protocol and legislation. The history of the kingdom arrived at its conclusion in dramatic fashion with the conquest of Ayutthaya by the Burmese, eternal enemies of the Tai, who had already succeeded in surrounding and attacking the capital in 1569, albeit for a brief period. In 1767 the ruins of the city, which had been sacked and burned to the ground, marked the climax of the Burmese invasion, but not the definitive defeat of the Tai, whose recovery would begin in the new capital, Thonburi, a few years later.

92 - THIS LARGE BRONZE HEAD (H. 17 IN/45 CM) IS ONE OF THE *PARÉ* TYPES OF BUDDHAS. THE IMAGES OF THE CROWNED BUDDHA BECAME PARTICULARLY WIDESPREAD IN THE 16TH CENTURY AT AYUTTHAYA (MUSÉE GUIMET, PARIS).

93 - THE HEAD OF THIS BRONZE BUDDHA WITH A TALL FLAME ON THE *USNISA* IS IN KEEPING WITH THE STYLISTIC CANONS OF THE MOST ANCIENT PERIOD OF THE AYUTTHAYA CIVILIZATION.

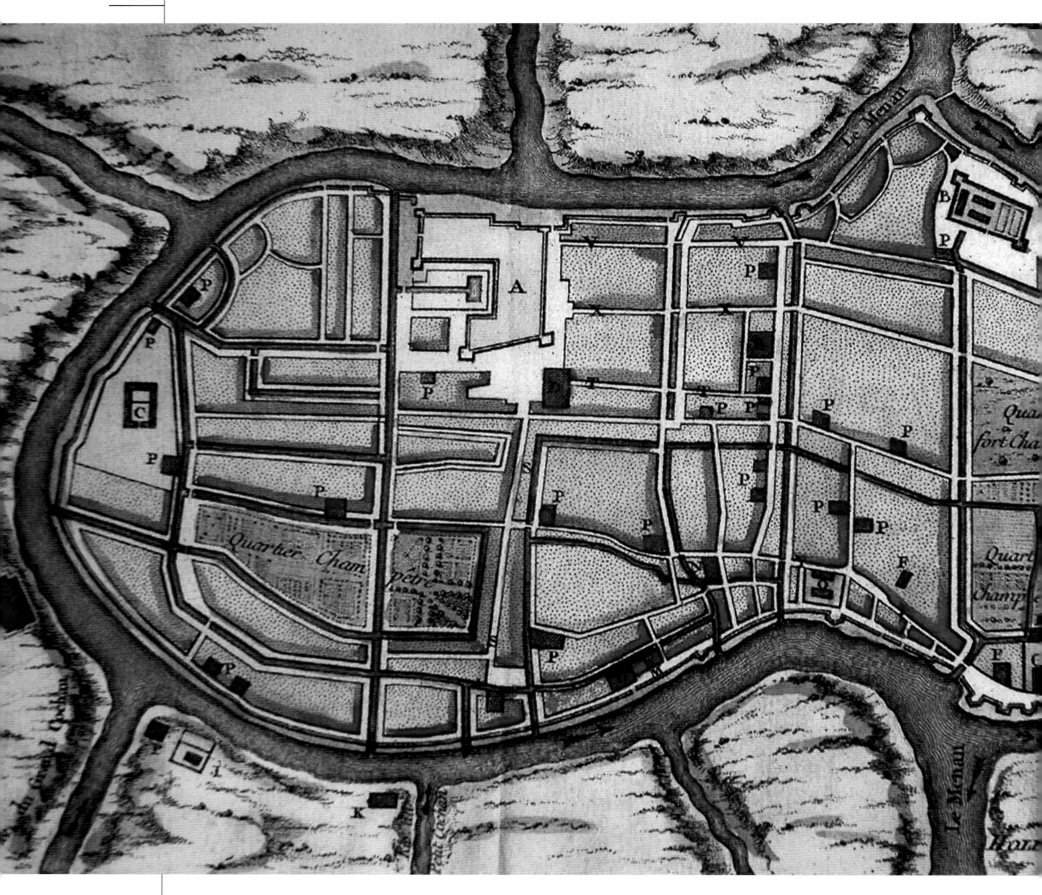

94-95 - THIS MAP, DRAWN UP IN
EUROPE IN THE 17TH CENTURY,
REPRODUCES A BIRD'S-EYE VIEW OF THE
CITY OF AYUTTHAYA IN PERSPECTIVE. ITS
CONFIGURATION AS AN ISLAND, FORMED

BY THE CONFLUENCE OF RIVERS AND
CANALS, IS QUITE EVIDENT, AS IS THE
RECTANGULAR LAYOUT OF ITS DISTRICTS,
WHICH ARE SEPARATED BY ARTIFICIAL
CANALS.

95 - AN AERIAL PHOTOGRAPH OF THE
SITE OF AYUTTHAYA IN WHICH ONE CAN
RECOGNIZE THE TWO MAIN ARCHITECTURAL
COMPLEXES IN THE CITY — WAT PHRA
MAHATHAT AND WAT RATCHABURANA.

Echelle de 600 Toises
100    200    300                    600

Except for the canals that passed through the city, marking out a network of rectangles, the layout of Ayutthaya was not in a regular grid pattern. The city was built at the confluence of the Chao Phraya, Lopburi and Pasak rivers and was transformed into an island by means of a canal that connected the Pasak and Lopburi rivers. The most important monuments, such as the royal palace and monastery, were built in the central-northern zones, and the first Buddhist complexes were constructed a short distance to the east. The settlements of the various East India Companies were located outside the city walls but in the immediate vicinity, southeast of the city. As we have already seen with other sites, here too the remains of civil architecture are scarce. There are three reasons for this: stone was used only in the construction of the religious monuments, while the lay edifices were made of wood with brick foundations, at least up to the 17th century; the capital was sacked by the Burmese and, up to the end of the 18th century, the building materials of the ruins were systematically removed to be used for the construction of Bangkok. Therefore, while there are no traces of the royal palace commissioned by Ramathibodi, we can still see the foundations of the Wang Luang. This palace was built by King Trailok in the second half of the 15th century in the northern district of the capital. Another part of the palace's brick walls was built by King Chakraphat in the mid-16th century. The palace housed the throne room and audience halls and was the residence of the royal family up to the time of the Burmese sacking. A monument of remembrance to the other buildings in the royal palace complex is provided by the Trimuk, a pavilion that was reconstructed in the 19th century over the foundations of the original structure. The most ancient monuments that have survived lie outside the city wall and date to the time of Prince U Thong. This period is best represented by Wat Phutthaisawan, which was built to the south in 1353, on the site of the temporary camp set up by U Thong before his coronation and before he moved to the royal palace. The peristyle court contains various restored statues of the seated Buddha, a Khmer style *prang* (restored in the 17th century), and the residence of the patriarch, which has some 17th-century wall paintings depicting the *jataka* and the footprints of Buddha. Another monument connected to U Thong is Wat Phanan Choeng, which was founded at the confluence of the Chao Phraya and Pasak rivers before construction work began in the capital.

In 1359 U Thong commissioned the building of Wat Chao Phya Thai to the east of the city, on the left bank of the Pasak, to accommodate a group of monks who had returned from Sri Lanka, where they had studied with a famous master. The complex was renamed Wat Yai Chai Mongkon when King Naresuan commemorated his victory over the Burmese in 1592. The bell-shaped *stupa* has the streamlined form typical of these structures in Ayutthaya, with a smaller *stupa* of the same type at each of the four corners. Thanks to recent restoration work, the soaring silhouettes of the *stupas* and *prangs* that dominate the Buddhist monasteries in the ancient capital bear witness to the golden age of Ayutthaya. The reliquary tower (*prang*) lies in the middle of the *wat*, and the other monuments stand around it, either aligned on the main East-West axis or arranged in a symmetrical pattern. This regular arrangement, a quest for a harmonious relationship between the monuments and the geometrical principles that govern the inner layout of the area, reflects the adoption of the spatial-architectural concepts of Khmer origin that the Siamese builders utilized for Buddhist architecture. Certain features were already present, to a certain degree, in the complexes of Sukhothai, but had been realized with less rigor than at Ayutthaya. The most evident result of this inspiration and influence lies in the delimitation of the holy area of the *wat* by means of concentric rectangular walls. Some of these were modeled on the gallery-boundary style so popular with the Khmer. Other effects seen are in the presence of lustral basins or moat-boundaries and in the importance attached to the *prang*, which, being the focal point of the entire complex, represents the fully achieved architectural and religious transformation of the ancient *prasat*. The sanctuary tower of Ayutthaya is, in fact, a commemorative monument of a funerary type similar to that of the *stupas* and *chedis* at Sukhothai. It serves as a reliquary, and houses, in a crypt within the foundation, the relics of Buddha, substitutes of his relics, or the ashes of a revered Buddhist master. Generally the *wihan* faces the east entrance of the *prang*, while the *bot* might be on the same axis, but is situated on the opposite side. The only remains of these edifices at Ayutthaya are the bases and columns that supported the wooden roofs, which also disappeared quite some time ago. The walls of these rectangular halls, made of bricks held together with mortar and coated with stucco, were probably interspersed with the typical vertical slits, and would have been either left completely white or lavishly decorated on the outside, depending on the fashion of the later period. An important role in the decoration of the edifices was played by the leaves of the entrance doors, which were made of wood that

was either engraved and gilded, inlaid with fragments of mirrors and mother of pearl, or simply lacquered. For the most part, the subjects represented were images of guardian divinities, protectors of the monastery, surrounded by floral motifs that might even be considered the main theme of the decoration. The rest of the interior of the *wat* is occupied by small *chedis* and *prangs* that were occasionally built next to the principal monuments. While the layout of the *wat* – at least during the Ayutthaya period – corresponds to an orderly, unitary organization of its various components, during the course of the following centuries, when the influence of the well-arranged Khmer plan was no longer so strong, the clarity of the original arrangement was lost amid the many new edifices built inside the complex.

96 - THE MINOR *STUPAS* OF
WAT YAI CHAI MONGKON
WERE PARTLY DEMOLISHED
WHEN AYUTTHAYA WAS
CONQUERED IN 1767.

96-97 - ALONG THE WALLS
THAT MARK THE PERIMETER
OF WAT YAI CHAI MONGKON
IS A LONG SERIES
OF RECENT STATUES
OF THE SEATED BUDDHA.

97 BOTTOM - AMONG THE
RUINS OF A *WIHAN* IN THE
ENCLOSURE OF WAT YAI
CHAI MONGKON IS THIS
LARGE STATUE OF A
RECLINING BUDDHA
COMMISSIONED BY KING
NARESUAN AND WHICH WAS
RECENTLY RESTORED.

98-99 - The ruins of a *wihan* and a *bot*, towered over by the central *prang*, lie on the main axis of Wat Phra Ram.

99 top - The roots of a centuries-old plant in Wat Phra Mahathat surround a stone head of Buddha, which has become a tourist attraction as well as place of veneration for the faithful.

99 bottom - Despite the fact that at first sight Wat Phra Mahathat seems to be a confused mass of buildings and ruins, its well organized layout eventually becomes quite clear.

101 - The center of Wat Ratchaburana is the square platform on which are the large central *prang* and the four corner *chedis*. Along the main axis of the complex, in front of the platform, are the remains of the walls of the *wihan*.

The first three complexes built in the 14th to 15th centuries (Wat Phra Ram, Wat Phra Mahathat and Wat Ratchaburana) exemplify the above-mentioned features, despite the fact that they were all rebuilt in a later period. They bear witness to the support that Theravada Buddhism continued to receive from the kings of Ayutthaya, as well as those of Sukhothai. Wat Phra Ram was constructed in 1369 and is articulated around the *prang* built on the site where Ramathibodi, the first king of Ayutthaya, was cremated. Despite the fact that the *prang* was rebuilt in the 15th and 18th centuries, the complex is still a fine example of the monastery architecture of the early period, with its references to Khmer spatial concepts and the importance attached to the central monument. The four *chedis* placed on the corners of the platform, supporting the reliquary tower, evoke the quincunx arrangement adopted at Angkor. The same tradition holds sway in the square enclosure with corner pavilions that surrounds the central group, as well as in the alignment of the *wihan* and the *bot* along the main axis. The name of King Borommaracha I (1370-1388) is on the other hand connected to Wat Phra Mahathat, one of the largest complexes in Ayutthaya, built in the second half of the 14th century but drastically rebuilt in the 18th century. After the most recent changes, the arrangement of the *wat* looks like that of the neighboring Wat Ratchaburana, but unlike this temple, the *prang* built in 1374 has not been preserved. Outside the enclosure that confined the platform of the *prang*, there are, respectively to the East and West, the remains of two symmetrical *bots*. Although the court contains minor *chedis* and *prangs*, its orderly layout is still quite recognizable.

The third of the most ancient Buddhist complexes in Ayutthaya is Wat Ratchaburana, which is particularly significant for the architectural remains, the important discovery made in 1957 inside the *prang*, and the history of its construction, which once again is connected to events concerning the ruling family. In fact, as Thai historic sources tell us, when King Intharacha died in 1424, two of his sons disputed the right to the throne by waging a duel on elephants, which ended with the tragic death of both of them. The third son was crowned king with the name of Borommaracha II and he ordered the construction of the monastery on the site where his two brothers had been cremated. Their ashes were then placed in the two chedis of Chao Aye and Chao Yi. The fact the King Borommaracha buried a large treasure inside the prang of Wat Ratchaburana may be interpreted as a meritorious act for the benefit of his two brothers. As was mentioned above, the objects in this treasury were found in 1957, when some thieves were caught violating the underground chamber of the prang and stealing many gold artifacts. They were found in the so-called treasure chamber, a room hidden under another chamber that, in turn, had been hewn out of the rock under the floor of the prang cella. The treasure chamber had a niche in each of its four walls to contain the artifacts. Unfortunately, after the theft it was impossible to reconstruct the order of their original placement. Curiously enough, the thieves did not notice that there was a third chamber under the laterite floor of the second one. This was discovered some time after the attempted burglary, and yielded a gold reliquary in the shape of a stupa, decorated with precious stones that had been placed inside other reliquaries made of iron, copper and silver. The body of the objects found at this site is unique both for the material employed and the workmanship of most of them. Besides the many statuettes of Buddha sculpted in different ages and in different Buddhist countries, the treasure consists of various gold objects representing miniature royal symbols. This includes a small shoe, a parade elephant, a ceremonial sword with its sheath, a crown, bracelets and other items such as goose-shaped perfume receptacles, small plaques in the shape of fantastic animals, and embossed images of Buddha.

But Wat Ratchaburana also houses another treasure of inestimable value: the most ancient examples of Buddhist painting ever found inside a temple. The placement inside the crypt, where they would be hidden and protected, not only spared the paintings from destruction during the Burmese sacking of the city, but also preserved them from the humid climate of the area, which would certainly have ruined them had they been exposed to the air outside. Thus we have the only document that allows us to imagine what the decoration of the interior of 15th-century *wats* must have been like, since previously only fragments had been preserved in a building in Wat Putthaisawan, and these only dated to the 17th century. Wat Ratchaburana paintings are on the walls of the first and second chambers. The former depict semi-divine beings and figures of guardians with Chinese facial features painted in two very different styles and combined in such a way that their meaning is difficult to grasp. The paintings in the 'treasure chamber' are arranged in horizontal chronicles and represent episodes from the life of Buddha, scenes of the *jataka*, the eighty great disciples and the Buddhas of the past, highlighted against a red background that has bright and colorful gold leaf decoration. The figures of the disciples, depicted in three-quarter views, are defined in a very thin, regular and interrupted outline that reminds one of the pattern of the tiles in Wat Si Chum at Sukhothai. However, they surpass those compositions because of the greater freedom and skill in rendering the groups and the relationship between the figures. Wat Ratchaburana is situated next to Wat Mahathat and has a surface area equivalent to that of the latter. Aligned on the East-West axis are the *wihan*, the central platform with the *prang*, and the *bot*, in this order; while smaller *stupas* and *wihans* are placed symmetrically at either side of the axis. The *prang* is the best ancient example of this type of structure, having features of all the reliquary towers of the time. The monument stands in the middle of an elevated square platform, with four *chedis* placed at the corners. The tower rests on an elevated base and has the typical curved profile of the Ayutthaya *prang*. The denticular layout that is repeated on the layers of the spire is heightened by the presence, on every corner, of a lanceolate antefix that accentuates the vertical thrust of the monument. The cornice of the doors in the three false entrances placed at the cardinal points once bore an image of a stucco-coated standing Buddha. A steep stairway leads from the base of the platform to the entrance of the relic chamber. The side walls of the main *wihan*, which are made of bricks, and part of the three-entrance façade have been preserved. In the interior one can see the fragments of the cylindrical brick pillars arranged in two rows that once supported the wooden roof. One can still get an idea of the original appearance of the pillars in Wat Yai Chai Mongkon; stuccoed and crowned with the characteristic lotus-bud capitals.

102 - TAPERED ANTEFIXES, SEMI-DIVINE
BEINGS, FORBIDDING GUARDIANS, AND
*GARUDAS* WITH OUTSPREAD WINGS FACE
ONE ANOTHER ALONG THE DENTICULAR
SPIRE OF WAT RATCHABURANA *PRANG*.

103 - WAT RATCHABURANA CONTAINS
*STUPAS* IN DIFFERENT ARCHITECTURAL
STYLES. THE TEMPLE WAS BUILT AT THE
BEHEST OF KING BOROMMARACHA II IN
THE 15TH CENTURY.

104 - The paintings in the Treasury Hall of Wat Ratchaburana are organized on different registers. The figures have a black outline, are painted against a red ground, and have gold leaf decoration.

104-105 - The paintings in Wat Ratchaburana were executed with the secco technique. In the upper part of the niche, a pair of birds flanking a tree dominates the *jataka* scenes below them.

106 left - This gold repoussé plaque, part of the treasure of Wat Ratchaburana, depicts the standing Buddha performing the *abhayamudra* gesture (Chao Sam Phraya National Museum, Ayutthaya).

106 right - This group of objects found in the reliquary chamber of Wat Ratchaburana includes numerous gold and silver repoussé votive tablets (Chao Sam Phraya National Museum, Ayutthaya).

107 - The most common image of the Enlightened One among the treasures in Wat Ratchaburana portrays his victory over Mara, in which Buddha is seated, performing the *bhumisparsamudra* gesture (Chao Sam Phraya National Museum, Ayutthaya).

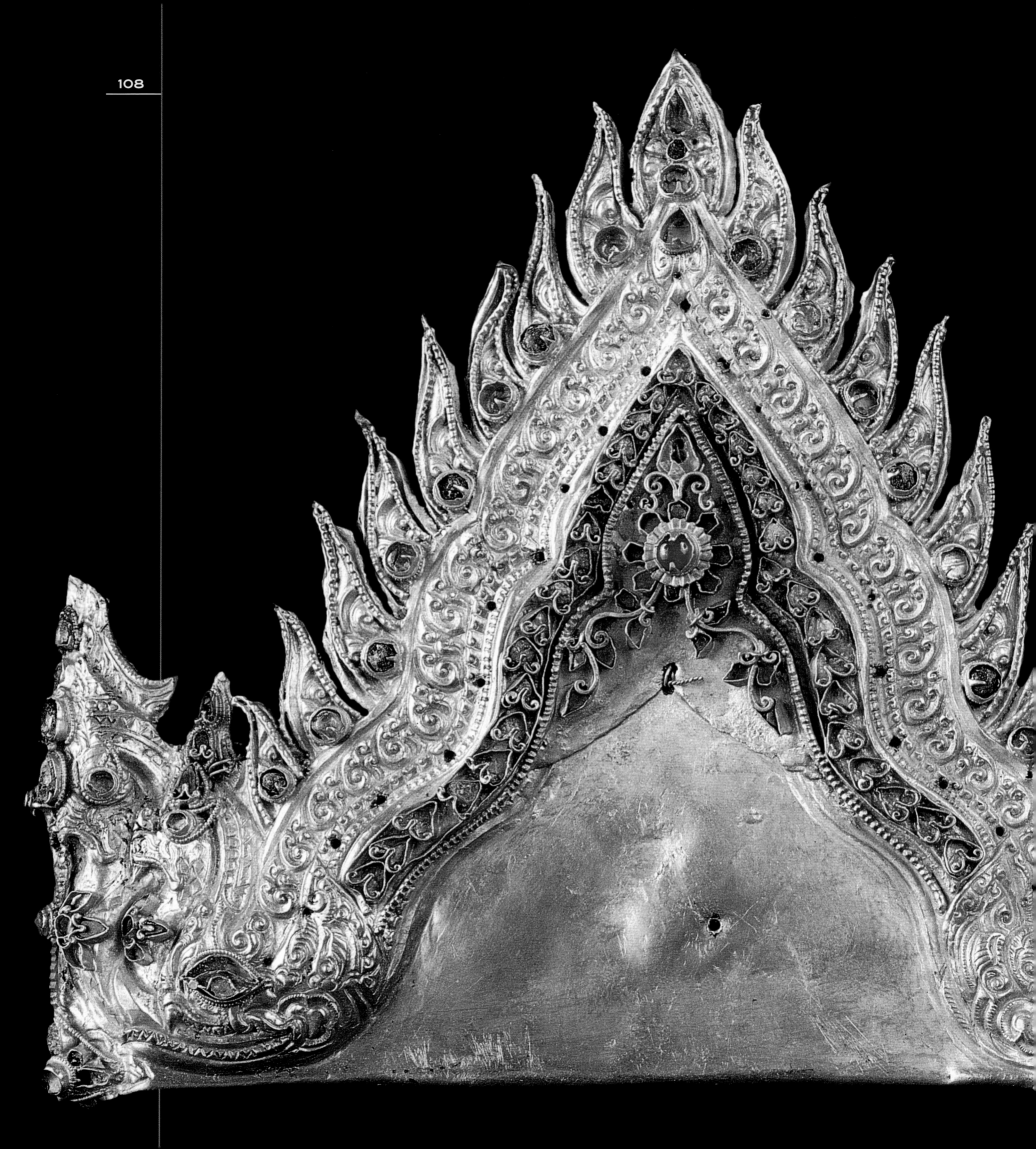

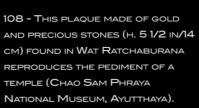

108 - This plaque made of gold and precious stones (h. 5 1/2 in/14 cm) found in Wat Ratchaburana reproduces the pediment of a temple (Chao Sam Phraya National Museum, Ayutthaya).

109 - Among the objects found in the Treasury of Wat Ratchaburana was this finely wrought tiered antefix (Chao Sam Phraya National Museum, Ayutthaya).

110 AND 111 CENTER - WAT
RATCHABURANA HAS BOTH
RELIGIOUS AND SECULAR
OBJECTS. THE LATTER ARE
MOSTLY ROYAL REGALIA, SUCH
AS THE TWO FANS SHOWN HERE,
ORNAMENTS SUCH AS THE TWO
GOLD BRACELETS, OR LUXURY
UTENSILS (CHAO SAM PHRAYA
NATIONAL MUSEUM,
AYUTTHAYA).

111 TOP AND BOTTOM - THIS
CEREMONIAL SWORD WITH A
GOLD SHEATH AND PRECIOUS
STONES WAS, LIKE THE SLIPPER,
PART OF THE ROYAL TREASURE IN
THE WAT RATCHABURANA
COMPLEX (CHAO SAM PHRAYA
NATIONAL MUSEUM,
AYUTTHAYA).

112 - WAT RATCHABURANA ALSO HAS VARIOUS OBJECTS DEPICTING ANIMALS, SUCH AS THIS EXQUISITE SMALL GOLD ELEPHANT DECORATED WITH SEMI-PRECIOUS STONES (CHAO SAM PHRAYA NATIONAL MUSEUM, AYUTTHAYA).

113 - THIS GOLD RELIQUARY IN THE SHAPE OF A *STUPA* (H. 10 IN/26.5 CM) WAS FOUND IN WAT RATCHABURANA AND CONTAINED THREE OTHER PRECIOUS IMAGES (CHAO SAM PHRAYA NATIONAL MUSEUM, AYUTTHAYA).

During the second half of the 15th century there was a shift in taste toward the Sukhothai style at the expense of the Khmer influence. This resulted in a different arrangement of the interior of the *wat*, as the bell-shaped *stupa* with four jutting avant-corps replaced the *prang* in the middle of the complex. An example of this new tendency is the royal chapel known as Wat Phra Si Sanphet. Built as a royal temple in 1448 (or 1491) in the zone of the ancient royal palace (Wang Luang), the monastery was enlarged by Ramathibodi II in order to house the two *stupas* that contained the ashes of his father, Trailok, and his elder brother, Borommaracha III. Later, in 1530, a third *stupa* was built to house the ashes of Ramathibodi II himself. The three reliquaries look like Ayutthayan campaniform *stupas* and have a taller, denticular base that supports the elongated bell-shaped body. A recently formulated theory suggests that the three *stupas* of Wat Phra Si Sanphet were built after the 17th century, as they do not appear in a Dutch view of the city that was painted in 1690. In 1499, Ramathibodi II also commissioned the construction of a *wihan,* opening eastward that was to house a gilded bronze statue of the standing Buddha. This sculpture, called Phra Si Sanphet, was ruined during the time of the 1767 Burmese invasion and was later transported by King Rama I to Wat Pho in Bangkok. The beautiful bronze statue from Phra Phuttha Sihing, now on show in the National Museum, Bangkok, also came from the Ayutthaya monastery. Some examples of the elegance of the architectural adornments are kept at the Chao Sam Phraya Museum in Ayutthaya. They are the beautiful wooden leaves of the doors of the *wihan* and of one of the *stupas*, which represent a pair of guardians in a symmetrical position, mirroring each other. The dates of manufacture are unclear; either dating to the end of the 15th century or the beginning of the 16th century or as some experts state, the late 17th or first half of the 18th century. A cruciform edifice (*prasada*) crowned by a pyramidal *chedi* ended the row of monuments to the west, as a sort of counterpart to the *wihan* that preceded the east entrance.

114 - THE WOODEN DOOR LEAFS DECORATED WITH RELIEFS OF A PAIR OF GUARDIAN DIVINITIES COME FROM WAT PHRA SI SANPHET (CHAO SAM PHRAYA NATIONAL MUSEUM, AYUTTHAYA).

114-115 - THREE BELL-SHAPED *STUPAS* IN WAT PHRA SI SANPHET FLANKED BY THE REMAINS OF THREE *MONDOPS*.

The first half of the 17th century appears to be marked by a return to the Khmer architectural style. This is epitomized by Wat Chaiwatthanaram, the complex built in 1630 by King Prasat Thong to commemorate his dead mother, as well as to legitimate, in some way, his ascension to the throne as a usurper. In the middle of the enclosure of the *wat* we again see a *prang*, surrounded by other smaller ones. However, the special quality of this complex lies in the eight conical towers that imitate the wooden structures in the shape of a mountain used in the royal cremations and which in the 17th century were sometimes more than 328 ft (100 m) high. These towers have an octagonal plan and the shape of a slender pyramid with a concave profile, and their arrangement on the platform is in keeping with a particular geometric pattern seen in Khmer temples. By means of these explicit symbolic references, the monument celebrated at once the pious behavior of the king, for building Buddhist temples, and his glory as a universal ruler who governs from the center of such a well-organized space. During the reign of King Narai, the second half of the 17th century witnessed the construction of the first civil constructions made entirely of brick. Although nothing remains of the royal palace commissioned by this king, a glimmer of what the royal residence must have looked like can be gleaned from the palace of King Narai at Lopburi (Narai Ratchaniwet). It was built in 1665 but restored and enlarged in the mid-19th century by King Mongkut. Despite a certain degree of restoration work done in the 18th and 19th centuries, Wat Na Phra Men offers the opportunity to admire one of the most beautiful examples of the late monastic architecture of Ayutthaya, which already heralds the style that dominated the first Bangkok period. The *wihan* dates to the first half of the 19th century, while the *bot* has retained its 17th-century plan, with its thick and impressive masonry structure, sloping roof with superposed, recessed levels, and external columns on the longer sides supporting the slopes of the roof. Equally characteristic features are the lozenges along the side walls of the hall and the broad portico that dominates the main entrance of the temple.

116 AND 116-117 - THE CONSTRUCTION OF
WAT CHAIWATTHANARAM IN THE 17TH
CENTURY AT THE BEHEST OF KING PRASAT
THONG MARKED A RETURN TO KHMER

INFLUENCES IN THE ARCHITECTURE OF
AYUTTHAYA. THIS AERIAL VIEW CLEARLY
SHOWS THE CENTRAL *PRANG*,
SURROUNDED BY EIGHT CONICAL TOWERS.

Besides the monuments built in the capital, the Ayutthaya style is represented by other buildings in different provinces that are anything but secondary from an artistic standpoint. An example of this is Wat Yai Suwannaram at Phetchaburi, a town southwest of Bangkok along the Gulf of Thailand. This complex dates from the first half of the 17th century and, despite the 19th-century restoration work, has maintained all the features of the original style. This monument is known above all for the ancient paintings in the *bot* depicting divinities and supernatural beings (*yaksha*, *garuda* and *naga*), arranged in horizontal lines, all facing towards the statue of Buddha at the end of the hall. Floral and flame motifs fill the spaces between one figure and another. The palette is prevalently white and red, while black is used for the finishing touches on the jewels and clothes, which appear to be carefully executed. Compared to earlier paintings, one notes an increase in the size of the compositions, greater assurance in the rendering of the faces and in the arrangement of the figures in the space, and a more skillful use of colors. As a whole, these factors led to great decorative as well as descriptive efficacy. Similar sensitivity can also be seen in the paintings of the *bot* in Wat Ko Kaeo Suttharam at Phetchaburi, which were completed in 1734 and represent episodes in the life of Buddha. Traces of the influence of Chinese painting can be detected in the rendering of the landscape, while the iconography seems to adhere to local tradition and reflect the gestures and postures of traditional Thai dance. Again, in Wat Phra Si Ratana Mahathat at Phitsanulok, which lies on the site of an earlier *wat*, there is a 14th-century *prang* and a *wihan* rebuilt in the 18th century. In the interior of this monument is the Phra Phuttha Chinarat, the famous monumental gilded bronze statue of the seated Buddha, which was accomplished in the 15th century.

118-119 - THE WALL PAINTINGS OF THE *BOT* IN WAT KO KAEO SUTTHARAM AT PHETCHABURI DATE BACK TO 1734 AND ARE A PRECIOUS EXAMPLE OF AYUTTHAYA PAINTING.

120-121 - The horizontal registers of the paintings in Wat Yai Suwannaram at Phetchaburi are separated from one another by bands with plant motifs, while the individual figures are inserted in zigzag patterns, among which there are paintings of floral compositions.

121 - Various divine figures animate the walls of the BOT in Wat Yai Suwannaram at Phetchaburi. These personages, who face the statue of Buddha in the hall, are painted in horizontal registers dominated by white with touches of red in the background.

122 AND 123 - LIVELY SCENES FROM THE LIFE OF BUDDHA ARE PAINTED ON THE WALLS OF THE *BOT* IN WAT KO KAEO SUTTHARAM AT PHETCHABURI IN TRIANGULAR SPACES SEPARATED FROM ONE ANOTHER BY PAINTED REPRODUCTIONS OF *STUPAS*.

# THE HISTORY OF NORTH THAILAND

The history of the Haripunchai kingdom – named after the former capital, present-day Lamphun – marks another important stage in the multiform cultural past of Thailand, since it bears witness to the last carryover of the Mon tradition, which had spread from Lopburi to the north around the 8th century. The historic events regarding the foundation of the Haripunchai kingdom are sheathed in legend. The legend tells of the marriage of a local hermit, the founder of the city of Haripunchai, and a Mon princess sent from the plains to govern the northern territories. Implicit in this fantastic tale is the actual expansion of Dvaravati, which probably took place at some point between the 8th and 9th centuries and resulted in the foundation of a *muang* that thrived independently up to the 13th century. The spread of Theravada Buddhism in the northern territories of Thailand is also a feature of the Dvaravati kingdom. The history of Haripunchai continued without any traumatic events right up to the 11th century, when the expansionist policy of the Khmer led them to this small northern kingdom, undermining its peaceful existence. After the first attack of the army of Lopburi, which had become a major

Khmer city, around the year 1050, Haripunchai was struck by a cholera epidemic, after which the population abandoned the city. The residents took refuge first at Thaton and later at Pegu, merging with the Mon people of southern Burma. This bond between Lamphun, Thaton and Pegu was maintained beyond these times and became a major path for the revival of Buddhism through the contact they had with the Theravada community in Sri Lanka. After this crisis had passed there was another attack by the Khmer during the reign of the Mon king Aditya, who was celebrated for resisting the siege and thwarting the enemies. The Haripunchai kingdom continued to flourish for some time, while Khmer power was becoming weaker and the *muang* of Sukhothai and Chiang Rai were emerging. The latter was the power center of one of the Tai groups that, like the Sukhothai, had settled in the central-northern regions of Thailand. Chiang Rai, founded in 1262, was the new capital of the kingdom of King Mangrai, who in 1281 conquered

Haripunchai and extended his dominion over the entire northern region, giving rise in 1296 to the kingdom of Lan Na with the foundation of the 'new capital,' Chiang Mai. The cultural links with the Buddhist civilization of the central plains were profound and had quite an impact on the early history of Haripunchai. However, this civilization also assimilated other influences through its contacts with the neighboring Mon population of Burma, relations with northeastern India, and lastly, the arrival of the Tai. The artistic heritage of the Mon culture is only preserved in the ancient capital of the kingdom, Lamphun (Haripunchai). This city, like the other Mon settlements of Lampang and Phrae, had the typical oval plan, was bounded by a moat (that can still be seen) and was defended by bastions. The remaining monuments, together with the sculpture of Haripunchai, are an emblem of northern Mon culture and differ from all other Buddhist architecture in Thailand. These are tall, five-story pyramid-shaped towers, each of which is decorated with three niches per side and topped by a spire. Known as a *ratna-cetiya*, or 'stupa-jewel,' this type of monument has puzzled scholars, who are still searching for possible prototypes and have not yet come up with a satisfactory answer. In fact, some scholars have put forward the theory that structures of this type were widespread among the Mon of Dvaravati, but the finds that have survived to this day are too fragmented to allow for a clear reconstruction of the model for the *ratna-cetiya*. However, it may be that the pyramidal tower of Haripunchai is a re-elaboration of the temple of the Mahabodhi at Bodhgaya, in northeast India. Its origin is still unknown, but the local success of this monument is well documented by a series of pyramidal *chedi* that imitated its shape from the 13th to the 15th century. Among these is the *chedi* in Wat Phra That Haripunchai of Lamphun itself, built in 1418, and Wat Chedi Liam, constructed at the end of the 13th or beginning of the 14th century at Wiang Kum Kam near Chiang Mai. Also worthy of note is a *chedi* with a similar shape built inside Wat Mahathat at Sukhothai and the *chedi* in Wat Phya Wat at Nan, whose date is uncertain.

124 - A *kinnari* decorates the roof of Wat Phra Kaeo Don Tao at Lampang.

126 - The five-level pyramid-shaped profile of Wat Chedi Liam.

127 left - Miniature reproductions of *chedis* line the various stories of Wat Chedi Liam.

127 right - A stucco lion guards the area between Chedi Liam and the *wihan*.

One of the most ancient examples is the 13th-century Wat Kukut at Lamphun. The principal *chedi* is a pyramid with a square base, more than 66 ft (20 m) tall, and consisting of five levels of decreasing height with three niches per side and small *chedis,* imitating the form of the pyramidal tower, that were placed on the corner of each level. Information gathered from an inscription tells us that the *chedi*, made of bricks and laterite and with stucco decoration, probably dates from the mid-12th century, but in 1281 it was restored after earthquake damage. Each of the 60 niches contains a terra cotta statue of Buddha, made from a mold and coated with stucco,

a technique that was particularly well developed in the kingdom of Haripunchai and was maintained in Lan Na art. The statues in the niches, which are of decreasing size from one level to the next, depict the standing Buddha with his left arm hanging by his side and right hand in a variation of the *abhayamudra* position, with the palm facing outward and held close to the chest. These works epitomize the Haripunchai style, which grew out of the matrix of the Mon tradition of Dvaravati which, with the addition of Burmese and Khmer elements, produced a synthesis that is extremely interesting from an aesthetic standpoint.

128 TOP - SMALL *CHEDIS* DOT THE AREA OF WAT PHRA THAT HARIPUNCHAI AT LAMPHUN.

128 BOTTOM LEFT - WAT KUKUT'S *CHEDI* HAS FIVE LEVELS.

128 BOTTOM RIGHT - A SMALL *CHEDI* LIES IN THE VICINITY OF THE MAIN TOWER OF WAT KUKUT.

129 - THE NICHES OF WAT KUKUT'S *CHEDI* HOUSE STATUES OF BUDDHA.

130-131 AND 131 - THE WARM COLOR OF
THE STUCCO ENLIVENS THE SYMBOLIC
GESTURES OF THE STATUES OF BUDDHA
SITUATED IN THE NICHES OF WAT
KUKUT'S *CHEDI* AT LAMPHUN. THE PALM
OF THE RIGHT HAND FACING OUTWARD
INDICATES PROTECTION OR ALLEVIATION.

The statuary consists mostly of images of the standing Buddha, but there are also statues of the seated Enlightened One; the materials mostly used for these works were terra cotta and stucco and, to a lesser degree, bronze. The basis of these creations were the Dvaravati faces of Buddha, as the Haripunchai ones have the same continuous triple arch of the eyebrows, half-lowered eyelids and mouth with thick lips. Given this common basis, the originality of the Haripunchai artistic output was manifested with variations that give rise to diverse discoveries, each of which emphasizes, with a different degree of intensity, one of the common features of the entire group. The innovations consist of the following: the form of the eyelids, which, although always half-lowered, are rendered with a straight line in the upper part and a curved line in the lower one; the arch of the eyebrows, which is very undulated; the rather square shape of the face, which in some cases becomes wider on a level with the temples; the straight or only slightly undulated profile of the thin band that borders the hair; the stylization of the curls, which move in a rather pronounced conical spiral; the protuberance on the head (*ushnisha*) surmounted by a small conical jewel; and, once again, the presence in some statues of a thin line above the upper lip to indicate a moustache. The rendering of the garment is a combination of the Dvaravati tradition, characterized by the long mantle that covers both shoulders and forms two groups of symmetrical folds in the lower part, and the Indian Pala school tradition. This arrived in Thailand by way of Burma and is manifested in certain details regarding the arrangement of the monastic frock. Together with the images of Buddha, the Haripunchai school of sculpture also depicted monks, Buddhist disciples

and figures in royal attire, in keeping with a caricature style that seems to have derived from a tendency of one part of ancient Dvaravati sculpture. An example of this is the beautiful terra cotta statue of a seated disciple in the *vajrasana* position with his hands joined on a level with his chest (*anjalimudra*). The exaggeration of each of the features described above lends an almost expressionistic intensity to the statue that is manifested in the face, which looks like a mask because of the globular, wide-open eyes and the simplified, pronounced lines of the mouth, the eyebrows and the folds of the neck. Lastly, mention must be made of the beautiful statues of Buddha, ornamented with a crown and regal attributes, which were created in the 11th century and are among the most ancient examples of this type of sculpture in Thailand. Next to the pyramidal *chedi* in Wat Kukut is another *chedi*, which also dates to the 13th century. However, unlike the former it does not seem that this type was imitated in Lan Na art. Made of bricks, the *chedi* has an octagonal base on which stands a very tall section with eight niches containing statues of Buddha, followed by another section that has been only partly preserved. The beautiful statues of the standing Buddha reveal all the distinguishing features typical of Haripunchai iconography: the hair in the form of small cones, separated from the face by a tubular band; exceptionally elongated ear lobes; conjoined eyebrows that describe a triple arch; half-lowered eyelids and slightly triangular eyes. The architectural ornamentation over the trilobate arches of the niches features flames or lanceolate elements, typical of the classical architecture of Pagan, while a different form, perhaps of Khmer inspiration, appears above the niches in the other *chedi*.

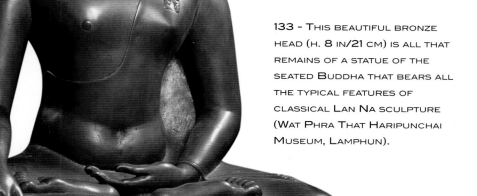

Although historical sources tell us that the foundation of Wat Phra That Haripunchai dates to the mid-12th century, none of its numerous monuments were built before the 15th century. According to custom, the most important monastery of Lamphun was supposedly founded at the behest of King Aditya, who had it constructed – in the shape of a *prasada*, temple – in order to house the relics of Buddha. Later, the reliquary was placed in another monument built in the 13th century, which in turn was incorporated into the *stupa* we see today, which dates from the mid-15th century. The *stupa* stands behind the *wihan*, occupying the central part of the monastery and extending upward for over 130 ft (40 m). This monument is a fine example of a classical type of Lan Na *stupa*, modeled on the campaniform one in Sukhothai, but with some modifications. One characteristic feature of Lan Na *stupas* is the monumental square base, formed by the superposition of sloped, notched steps, which in turn support other round steps of gradually decreasing size that were already employed in the architecture of

Sukhothai. The next element, consisting of the triple cornice with a round base – which to a certain extent was already present at Sukhothai – is here fully developed and supports the campaniform body of the *stupa*. The *stupa* is surmounted by a tapered spire featuring an umbrella crown that was added in a later period. The body of the *stupa* is dressed with the typical gilded copper plates that cover the most important reliquaries and is decorated with flowers in relief that alternate with images of the walking Buddha, which are now sadly, only partly preserved. An enclosure delimits the *stupa* area from the rest of the monastery, which contains the main *wihan* opening eastward, two other smaller *wihans* arranged symmetrically on the sides of the East-West axis, and other buildings, including the scripture library (*ho trai*) and a *ratna-cetiya*-style *chedi*. This tall brick structure with superposed levels is a replica of Wat Kukut *chedi*, which, like its model, is five stories high and culminates in a spire. Each story is decorated in similar fashion with niches that once contained images of Buddha.

134 - THE FINE STATUES OF THE SEATED BUDDHA IN THE PRAYER HALLS OF WAT PHRA THAT HARIPUNCHAI ARE PART OF THE LAVISH DECORATION CONSISTING OF IMITATION NICHES AND FACADES OF RELIGIOUS EDIFICES.

135 - THE SHAPE OF THE *STUPA* OF WAT PHRA THAT HARIPUNCHAI IS

THE RESULT OF SEVERAL ENLARGEMENT PROJECTS, THE LAST OF WHICH DATES FROM THE MID-15TH CENTURY.

136-137 - *CHO FA* ARE ELEMENTS OF TRADITIONAL THAI ARCHITECTURE THAT IN THIS CASE DECORATE THE ROOF OF THE *WIHAN* OF WAT PHRA THAT HARIPUNCHAI AT LAMPHUN.

138-139 - THE *PRANG* AND *CHEDI* OF WAT SI RATANA MAHATHAT NEAR SATCHANALAI ARE MADE OF BLOCKS OF LATERITE. THEY WERE CONSTRUCTED IN THE BAYON STYLE AND MAY DATE TO THE BEGINNING OF THE AYUTTHAYA ERA.

139 - TWO LARGE STATUES OF THE SEATED BUDDHA OCCUPY THE SITE OF ONE OF THE TWO *WIHANS* OF WAT SI RATANA MAHATHAT. IN THE 15TH CENTURY THE DOMINION OF KING TILOKA OF CHIAG MAI EXTENDED AS FAR AS SI SATCHANALAI.

The capture of Haripunchai and the successive birth of the Lan Na kingdom not only marked the end of the ancient Mon kingdom, but also the rise of the Tai population, which from that time on became the majority ethnic group in the northern domain. The creation of Lan Na was the result of the political ability of Mangrai, who in 1287 entered into an alliance with the leaders of the two main groups of the time: Rama Kamhaeng, who ruled over Sukhothai, and Ngam Muang, who governed the most ancient Thai principality, Phayao. After conquering Haripunchai and Lampang, Mangrai settled first at Wiang Kum Kam and in 1296 moved to Chiang Mai, the new capital in the middle of the northern territories, where he ruled up to his death in 1317. During his reign Mangrai did not limit his activity to the mere support of the Buddhist religion, but devoted his energy to spreading the orthodox form of Singhalese Buddhism. He involved the entire population in this operation and thus established in the north one of the bases of the future Thai identity. The history of the kingdom in the 14th and 15th centuries was marked by continuous strife with the neighboring *muangs*, especially Ayutthaya, which kept the northern kingdom engaged for many years. The conflict pitted the strongest Tai kingdoms of the time against one another: both Ayutthaya and Lan Na had succeeded in transforming themselves into kingdoms with an innovative structure able to control their respective provinces, thanks to an efficient bureaucratic system for the mobilization of manpower. They administrated them by means of a law code that was decreed by the kings themselves. However, the institutional

structure was still based on the personal relationships the kings established in order to guarantee the loyalty of the local administrators: no sooner did these relationships begin to deteriorate, than the very structure of the state revealed all its fragility. The second half of the 15th century was the age of two great sovereigns: King Tiloka of Chiang Mai and King Borommatrailokanat (Trailok) of Ayutthaya, who waged a ruthless struggle for absolute hegemony over the Thai world, which by then was becoming larger and larger. The two rulers left no stone unturned, in their effort to achieve victory. In the end, Chiang Mai prevailed over Ayutthaya and King Tiloka momentarily extended the dominion of the Lan Na kingdom as far as Sukhothai and Satchanalai, initiating a period of peace and extraordinary artistic and cultural activity in his domain. But this period did not outlast the two kings, and at the beginning of the 16th century, the clashes between the two powerful neighbors resumed, even more intensely than before because the Burmese also entered the fray. The kingdom of Chiang Mai was crushed between the two opposing powers and was unable to put up any resistance. Chiang Mai was therefore ruled in turn by Burma and Ayutthaya from the mid-16th century up to the second half of the 18th century, when the Siamese finally recovered and, supported by the Chiang Mai army, managed to drive out the Burmese and liberate the northern territories. This reconquest marked the beginning of the rebirth of Lan Na, but not of its independence: in the 19th century, the northern territories gradually became part of the Kingdom of Siam and later, of modern-day Thailand.

140 - Wat Phra That Lampang Luang, in the vicinity of Lampang, has almost miraculously preserved its original 15th-century appearance, both in the *chedi*, which has no gilding, and the impressive prayer hall (*wihan*) open on all four sides.

Lan Na represented the third great Thai artistic tradition, which developed together with Sukhothai and Ayutthaya and, like these two, boasted extremely original features that are especially noteworthy in the monastic edifices, architectural decoration and sculpture. In general, the architecture of northern Thailand consisted mostly of wooden constructions, by far the favorite building material and the principal element in the buildings in the *wats*. It was used most comprehensively in the main hall of the complex, which in this case is the *wihan*, which is more important and larger than the *bot*. The Lan Na *wihan* is an edifice with a rectangular plan, with an entrance on one of the two shorter sides and a characteristic wooden roof. The hall could have very low walls made of stuccoed bricks or be open on three or even four sides, as is the case with the Nan Tam *wihan* in Wat Phra That Lampang Luang of Lampang. The roof, which is supported by a sophisticated system of corbels of probable Chinese origin and rests on four rows of wooden pillars, consists of overlapping tiles. Unlike the architecture in the central plains, the inclination of the lower roofs is different from that of the upper ones, which modifies the direction of the curve of the roofs, decreasing their verticality and emphasizing, on the other hand, their outward movement. Thus, the roof looks like a pair of outspread wings above the rectangular

hall, with the lower ones protruding past the low side walls, almost touching the ground. A series of hooks (*cho fa*), a typical feature of Lan Na architecture that was assimilated by that of Bangkok, serves as an apotropaic decoration of the crown of the roof, taking on the form of stylized, grotesque animals. The borders of the roof are delimited by elaborate crested wooden cornices in the shape of *nagas* whose heads are curved backward to the roof ridges; at times the head of the *naga* is replaced by the most simple local pattern, a stylized leaf. The external corbels, which may have either a structural or purely decorative function, also provide examples of variations on the theme of the *naga* or other mythological beings. The portico framing the main façade of the *wihans* and *bots* is a true masterpiece of northern wooden decoration. The façade, which is made of wood covered with red lacquer and gilded, consists of a tall central tympanum and two lower lateral half-tympana, decorated with rectangular panels or with fretwork. The three openings framed by pillars are decorated with pensile friezes depicting double arches (*kong khieu*) that recall Buddha's curved eyebrows. The platform that supports the *wihan* (as well as other minor buildings) may be low or slightly elevated, and in the latter case a stairway with balustrades in the shape of *nagas*, a reminder of Khmer art, leads to the main entrance.

141 LEFT - THE INTERTWINED TAILS
OF TWO *NAGAS* FRAME THE ENTRANCE
TO WAT PHRA THAT LAMPANG LUANG.

141 RIGHT - A MONUMENTAL PORTAL ON THE
EAST SIDE OF THE ENCLOSURE LEADS TO THE
INTERIOR OF WAT PHRA THAT LAMPANG LUANG.

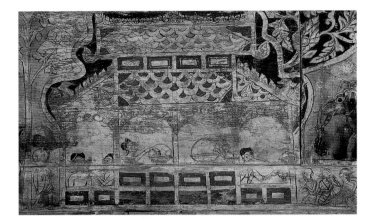

In the interior, the hall may have a nave with no aisle, or two side aisles marked off by rows of wooden pillars decorated with lacquer, gold leaf and pieces of colored glass. The ceiling may be open, revealing the corbel system that supports the roof, or be a lacunar, or coffered ceiling that entirely covers the hall. At the end of the *wihan*, the altar may take on the shape of a *ku*, which is a sanctuary similar to a miniature *prasat*, which is richly decorated and contains an image of Buddha. Inside the *wat* are other rather more typical edifices. One of these is the library (*ho trai*), which looks much like a small wooden *wihan*, built above a very tall platform in order to protect the palm-leaf manuscripts from the humidity. Lastly, the *wat* may also house shrines used to contain the footprints of Buddha (*buddhapada*), which are also kept in the *mondops* that often betray Burmese influence. As is the case elsewhere, the heart of the *wat* is either the *stupa* or the *chedi*, which in northern Thailand may take on different forms, depending on the prevailing style. Together with the *chedis* derived from the *ratna-cetiya* style of Haripunchai, the most popular form is the bell-shaped *stupa* of Sukhothai with some modifications. The final result is similar to that already described above at Wat Phra That Haripunchai in Lamphun. On the other hand, the Burmese influence can be noted in the *stupas* with their tall, square, fretted platform, mounted by the octagonal base that supports the body, which is smaller and has a concave profile. Other *chedis* seem to have assimilated other influences: northeastern India in the case of the *chedi* in Wat Chet Yot of Chiang Mai, and Yunnan in the *chedi* in Wat Ku Tao, also at Chiang Mai. The monuments that have survived in this city and the immediate surroundings are to be considered bona fide examples of northern Thai architecture, so much so that the Chiang Mai style has become synonymous with the architecture of the entire region.

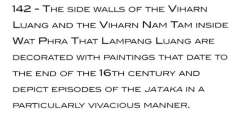

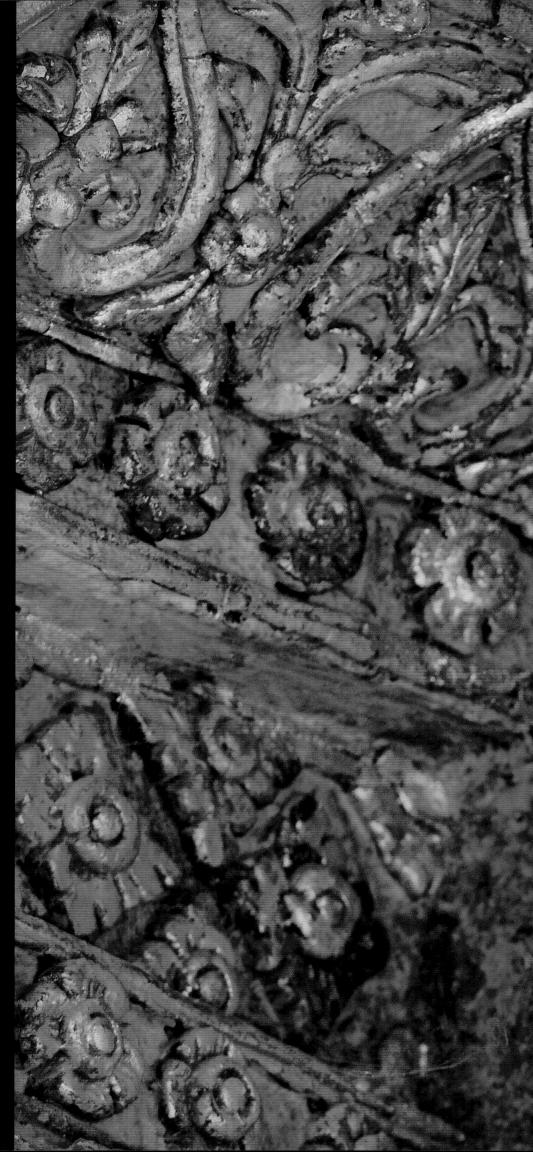

144-145 - GOLD LEAF DECORATION IS
WIDESPREAD IN BOTH ARCHITECTURE
AND SCULPTURE, AS CAN BE SEEN ON
THE FACE OF THIS SEMI-DIVINE FIGURE IN
WAT CHEDI LUANG OF CHIANG MAI.

The new city, built in 1296 on the bank of the Ping River in compliance with the scrupulous geomantic canons derived from Indian cosmology, was the capital of the Lan Na kingdom and experienced undulating fortunes, until 1892. Its square lay-out measured almost 1.2 miles (2 km) per side and the city had four entrances corresponding to the cardinal points, plus another entrance that was added later, on the south side. The bastions on the corners of the modern-day walls, which are surrounded by a moat, date to the 18th century and were recently restored. Inside the city walls, present-day Chiang Mai still has more than thirty temples. Some were rebuilt in recent times, while others, although they often include new monuments in their enclosures, house much older edifices in which the beauty of the original architecture is still evident. Such is the case with Wat Phra Singh, founded in 1345 with the construction of a *chedi* to house the ashes of a king and later enlarged with the addition of a *wihan* and other buildings. Whereas nothing remains of the original *chedi* and the present-day reliquary is a late 18th-century reconstruction, the charming library built on a miniature scale dates back to 1477. Erected on a tall base with stucco decoration consisting of semi-divine figures in different poses, this monument is a fine example of Lan Na wooden architecture; it underwent light restoration work in the 19th and 20th centuries. An equally important monument is Wihan Lai Kham, which stands beside the *chedi* and dates from the time the monastery was built (although it was recently slightly renovated). This structure, with its telescopic wooden roofs and low walls, houses the famous Phra Phuttha Sihing statue, which represents the late-15th-century northern Buddhist sculpture style (however, the head is a 20th-century copy). The interior has two cycles of 19th-century paintings that were restored in the early-20th-century and that illustrate non-canonical *jataka* stories. With an abundance of details and illustrated in a lively manner, the scenes reflect the settings and customs of everyday life in the 19th century with a very immediate style characterized by bright, contrasting colors that call to mind comic strips.

146 - THE TRADITIONAL STYLE OF NORTH THAILAND IS BEST EXPRESSED IN THE LIBRARY OF WAT PHRA SINGH AT CHIANG MAI, ELEVATED ON A TALL BASE IN ORDER TO PROTECT THE SACRED TEXTS FROM THE HOT AND HUMID CLIMATE.

146-147 - AN EXCELLENT EXAMPLE OF THE ARCHITECTURE OF LAN NA IS THE WIHAN LAI KHAM (LEFT), WHICH LIES INSIDE WAT PHRA SINGH AT CHIANG MAI. BUILT AT THE END OF THE 15TH CENTURY, IT HOUSES A VERY POPULAR STATUE OF BUDDHA.

148 AND 149 - STUCCO BAS-RELIEF
SCULPTURE REPRESENTING DIVINE
CREATURES (*DEVA*) AND INTRICATE

ORNAMENTAL MOTIFS ARE TO BE FOUND ON
THE TALL BASE OF THE LIBRARY (HO TRAI) IN
WAT PHRA SINGH AT CHIANG MAI.

Wat Chedi Luang, situated in the middle of the city, owes its importance to the fact that within its enclosure is the *lak muang*; the pillar of the city, believed to be the abode of the local tutelary genie that evokes the ancient animistic practices that were incorporated into the Buddhist tradition. The complex took on its present aspect after a long period that began in the 14th century, while the mid-15th century witnessed the beginning of the construction of the impressive brick and laterite *chedi*. This was completed during the reign of Tiloka and then collapsed due to

an earthquake in 1545. Wat Chiang Man, situated in the northern district of the city, not far from where the royal palace once stood, used to contain the most ancient *chedi* in Chiang Mai, which was built in 1297 by King Mangrai. The monument we see today is the result of the enlargement effected in 1471, when the *chedi* was converted into a typical bell-shaped *stupa* and dressed with gilded copper laminae. The base consists of a square platform with two steps, the first of which is decorated with a row of elephant heads and the second with niches that

150 - ALTHOUGH IT HAS LOST AROUND 98 FT
(30 M) OF ITS ORIGINAL HEIGHT BECAUSE OF
AN EARTHQUAKE, THE *CHEDI* OF WAT CHEDI
LUANG IS STILL IMPRESSIVE.

151 LEFT - FIVE *CHEDIS* AND A *STUPA* STAND
ON THE LATERITE AND BRICK BASE OF WAT
CHET YOT, ON WHICH ARE SCULPTED FIGURES
OF SEATED DIVINITIES.

open out on all four sides. Wat Phuak Hong, a monastery in the southwest corner of the ancient city, has a curious shape that some scholars claim might have derived from Yunnan architecture, while others think it is a round version of the pyramid-shaped *chedi* in Wat Kukut. Made of bricks in the 16th or 17th century, this monument rises for seven stories, each of which has niches on the walls where statues of Buddha were placed. Belonging to the same category is the *chedi* in Wat Rampoeng, an isolated monastery located a short distance west of the city. To the north, outside the city, lies Wat Ku Tao, which contains a curious 17th-century *chedi* consisting of overlapping, sloped spherical stories, each one decorated with four niches. According to Thai chronicles, the foundation of Wat Chet Yot, a large monastery outside the walls northwest of the city, took place during the period of splendor of Lan Na, during the reign of King Tiloka. The same source tells us that the construction of the temple coincided with the celebrations of the Eighth Buddhist Council, in 1477, which was devoted to the revision of the holy texts of the Pali canon. The monument that has made this com-

plex famous is a laterite and brick structure that is similar in some respects to the celebrated Maha-bodhi temple at Bodhgaya, in northeast India. The rectangular base supports a group of five pyramidal *chedis* in a quincunx arrangement and, in a more forward position, a campaniform *stupa*. One confirmation of the dating of this monument to the reign of Tiloka is provided by the stucco decoration on the walls, whose

style can be dated to the mid-15th century. Over 70 larger-than-life sized divinities are seated along the walls or standing on a level with the corners; they are modeled in high contours over brick armatures and placed on two registers, separated from one another by lozenges. The delicate facial features, especially of the standing statues, and the grace of the seated figures make these works true masterpieces of northern Thai art. Other examples of Lan Na architecture can be seen in the sites that became part of the kingdom, such as the ancient Mon city of Lam-

pang, which was established at the time of the Haripunchai kingdom and was conquered by Mangrai's troops at the end of the 13th century. The most ancient section of the city lies north of the Wang River, in the area that boasts one of the most famous monasteries, Wat Phra Kaeo Don Tao, which it is thought actually dates from the time of the Mon founder of the city. The fame of this site is connected to the most venerated statue of Buddha in Thailand, the so-called Emerald Buddha, the safeguard of the country, which is now in Wat Phra Kaeo in Bangkok. Having appeared at Chiang Rai in extraordinary circumstances in 1434, the statue was transported to Lampang, where it remained for 32 years before being transferred to Chiang Mai and, later on, to Laos. It remained there for over 200 years, first in Luang Phrabang and then Vientiane, until it was finally taken back to Bangkok in 1784. The statue is actually made of jadeite and has certain features of the Buddhist images that were popular in Lan Na in the 15th century; however, the date and actual origin of this work are extremely problematic. The rectangular enclosure of the monastery includes a *bot*, behind which

stands a tall bell-shaped *stupa* and, beside this, an elegant wooden *mondop*. The *mondop* has a cruciform plan, is open on all four sides, and is surmounted by a series of light pavilions that overlap in decreasing size, obviously derived from the corresponding Burmese *pyhatthats*. South of Wat Phra Kaeo Don Tao, but still inside its outer enclosure, is Wat Suchadaram, which has two especially interesting edifices: a *wihan*

and a *bot* built in the early 19th century whose wooden parts with intaglio decoration have retained all their elegance. It is also decorated with stucco friezes and fragments of inserted stained glass. In the west district of the city is Wat Pong Sanuk Thai, a temple dating from the late 18th century whose wooden *mondop* and other architectural details reveal a combination of the Lan Na and Burmese styles. The latter dated from the time when Lampang was occupied by the Burmese, from the mid-16th to the mid-18th century.

151 RIGHT - A *CHEDI* WITH AN INTERESTING ASPECT RISES UP IN WAT PHUAK HONG, AT CHIANG MAI, BUILT BETWEEN THE 16TH AND 17TH CENTURY. IT LOOKS LIKE THE

OCTAGONAL *CHEDI* IN WAT KUKUT, ALSO AT CHIANG MAI. EACH OF ITS SEVEN STORIES IS LINED WITH NICHES USED TO HOUSE STATUES OF BUDDHA.

More than 6 miles (10 km) west of the city, standing on a hill, is Wat Phra That Lampang Luang, a monastery that was part of one of the four fortified settlements (*wiang*) that protected the city during the Haripunchai period. This temple is considered to be the most beautiful in the Lan Na kingdom, as well as the most representative of northern Thai architecture. The precinct of the *buddhavasa*, bounded by an enclosure wall with an inner portico, is occupied by a main *wihan* and four minor ones, a *stupa*, a *bot*, a chapel to house Buddha's 'footprints,' and other minor buildings. A portal on the east side leads to the sacred precinct. The campaniform *stupa* dressed with gilded copper laminae, which stands behind the *wihan* on the East-West axis, imitates the structure of the northern monuments of this kind and was probably built in the mid-15th century over an earlier reliquary. The main hall of the *wat* is the Wihan Luang, made entirely of wood in 1476 and later restored without altering the original structure. The only changes were the wooden columns being replaced by others made of cement, and the flooring. This monument is open on all four sides and has four pitched and overlapping roof areas that descend and cover the entire hall. The interior contains a monumental *ku* displaying an image of Buddha in the back section, toward the west. To the left and right of the *ku* are the pulpit (*thammat*) and an elaborate candelabrum (*sattaphan*). North of the *stupa* is Wihan Nam Tam, which dates to the beginning of the 16th century and is most likely the oldest wooden edifice in Thailand. In a similar manner to the above-mentioned *wihan*, this is open on all four sides and in the interior, on a lovely altar framed with beams, is a statue of the seated Buddha. Traces of contemporaneous paintings appear on the inner wooden sections, offering an example of the most ancient artwork in northern Thailand, which was based on quintessential and very expressive draftsmanship. An extremely important sample of Lan Na painting can also be found at Nan, a city in the western area that was under the dominion of Sukhothai and, from 1443 on, under that of Chiang Mai. Prime examples are the *chedi* of Wat Chang Kham Wora Wihan, whose base has been decorated with the row of elephants typical of the Sukhothai *chedis* and the lotus blossom *chedi* of Wat Suan Tan, which has been altered by recent restoration. Other fabulous samples can be seen in the style of the statues of Buddha housed inside the local *wats*. Nowadays, while the artistic influence of the central plains is quite evident in the principal monuments in Nan, the expression of local art can be seen in Wat Phumin. This monastery founded in 1596 is built around the large cruciform hall that, like many edifices in this area, has the two-fold function of both a *wihan* and *bot*. Each of the four en-

trances is surmounted by a pyramidal roof much like that of the *mondop*, while the actual roof is of the interlocked type, supported by 12 wooden pillars decorated with red and black lacquer and gilt. On the inside walls are large paintings depicting stories of the *jataka* and episodes from the life of Buddha, divided into descriptive scenes much like those of Wat Phra Singh at Chiang Mai. Like Nan, the city of Phrae also became part of the kingdom of Lan Na during the reign of King Tiloka in the mid-15th century. Among the many *wats* that date from the 19th and 20th centuries and are interesting local variations of northern architecture, Wat Chom Sawan stands out for its marked Burmese influence, which imparts a particular appearance to the temple complex. The monastery, which dates from the early-20th century, consists of a main *wihan* made up of a series of wooden structures on

platforms that are connected to one another by lovely wooden roofs of different shapes and height. Outstanding among these are the overlapping roofs of the two structures that mark the entrances to the halls of the *wihan*. Chiang Saen, founded in 1327 or 1329 in the northernmost area of Thailand, was the birthplace of the first king of Lan Na and houses some remnants from the golden age of this kingdom. When the city was destroyed at the beginning of the 19th century, during the war against the Burmese, the temples were left alone. The campaniform *chedi* of Wat Phra That Chedi Luang, formerly the main monastery in the city, dates to the 14th century when Wat Pa Sak was likely to have been built. In the interior of the latter monument is a *chedi* with a special structure that combines the style of Wat Kukut at Lamphun with influences from Sukhothai.

152 - LIVELY SCENES FROM THE *JATAKA* (NARRATIVES OF THE PREVIOUS LIVES OF BUDDHA) ORNATE THE INTERIOR OF THE *BOT-WIHAN* IN WAT PHUMIN AT NAN, WHICH DATES BACK TO THE 16TH CENTURY.

152-153 - THE FOCAL POINT OF THE LARGE PRAYER HALL OF WAT PHUMIN OF NAN, WITH A CRUCIFORM PLAN, IS A QUADRUPLE REPRESENTATION OF BUDDHA IN THE *BHUMISPARSAMUDRA* POSITION.

5

---

# THE CHAKRI DYNASTY:
# FROM THONBURI TO BANGKOK

Protogonist of the rebirth of Ayutthaya after the Burmese attack of 1569 is King Naresuan (1555-1605), one of the few Tai rulers honored with the title of 'Great' because of his rare political and military prowess. Regaining the territory was not enough to ensure the solidity of the kingdom, which for the two following centuries was victim of instability due to repeated disputes over dynastic succession. Since there were no rules for succession to the throne, and since there were so many pretenders among the princes born of the king's numerous wives, every dispute was destined to become a tragic event and a political crisis that would jeopardize the stability of the kingdom. The constant conflict between the interests of the crown and personal interest within the various factions weakened the ancient Siamese kingdom from within, manifesting itself in all its gravity in the abortive mobilization of troops to defend the nation against the Burmese invasion of 1760. In 1767, immediately after the sacking, which was followed by the destruction of Ayutthaya and the deportation of Thai prisoners to Burma, the counteroffensive was led by a provincial governor, the future King Taksin, who reconquered the occupied territories and extended the borders of his new kingdom well beyond the preceding ones of Ayutthaya. Taksin then devoted his energy to the political reorganization of the country and laid the foundation for national rebirth, beginning with the new capital, Thonburi, on the right bank of the Chao Phraya River, in a opportune position facing the Gulf of Thailand in order to facilitate trade with China. The period of renewal initiated by Taksin ended in 1782 with his assassination by some rebels, who chose a new king, Ramathibodi (Rama I), a descendant of an ancient noble family from Ayutthaya who founded the Chakri dynasty. The death of Taksin also put an end to the brief duration of Thonburi, which was replaced by Bangkok as the new and definitive capital of Thailand. The city was founded in 1782 by King Rama I (1782-1809) on the left bank of the Chao Phraya River, opposite Thonburi but modeled on ancient Ayutthaya. In order to revive the splendor of the preceding capital, Bangkok was laid out over a labyrinth of canals, and the desire for restoration led to the scrupulous recovery of the symbols of the past: the ancient statues that had not been ruined or had been spared from Burmese destruction were taken to the new capital, while the new temples built to house them reflected the style of the monuments in Ayutthaya. The most significant and symbolic recovery was that of the statue of the Emerald Buddha which, according to one of the legends surrounding it, had been brought by Indra to the city of the gods, or had been carved out of an emerald that was part of the treasure of the king of the gods. In 1784 the statue, which had ended up in Laos, was transported to the new temple in Bangkok built by Rama I to house it, Wat Phra Kaeo. The temple stands on an artificial island that was the heart of the city, and its name – Ratanakosin, meaning 'the jewel of the gods' – derived directly from the presence of the statue. Wat Phra Kaeo is part of the Grand Palace complex, which was the center of the administrative and religious life of the kingdom, as well as the residence of the royal family until 1932. In his quest to retrieve the heritage of the past, Rama I set out to revive the precious, close relationship between the Buddhist religion and the state, which was indispensable for the existence of the new dynasty. The renewal of Siamese Buddhist monasticism, which had fallen into a state of doctrinal torpor and lax discipline, began with a series of laws promulgated by the king to reform the echelons of the religious community. This continued with the council whose purpose was to draw up an edition of the Buddhist law in the Pali language, as the preceding edition had disappeared during the 1767 looting. These reform measures, first undertaken by Rama I and continued by his successors, Rama II and Rama III, drew inspiration from the tradition of Sukhothai and Ayutthaya and emphasized the continuity between the new kingdom of Bangkok and the Tai culture that had preceded it. Vice versa, these measures left by the wayside the most distant past of Thai history, which had been so influenced by Khmer culture and Indian Brahmanic concepts. Only in the mid-19th century, during the reign of Mongkut (Rama IV), did the operation of rediscovering the lost aspects of Thai history begin. The policy thus initiated by this monarch was extremely important for 'Thai' cultural identity, which emerged during the course of this process. The rediscovery of the bonds of continuity with the Mon and Khmer traditions contributed to the reconstruction of the multi-faceted history of the country and created a consciousness of its cultural identity on a broader base than that of the past. It was also this consciousness that, after the fall of absolute monarchy in 1932, helped transform ancient Siam into the new nation of Thailand in 1939.

154 - THE *YAKSHA*, THE SPIRIT OF NATURE WITH A TERRIFYING ASPECT, OFTEN SERVES AS THE GUARDIAN OF PORTALS: THE ONE PHOTOGRAPHED HERE IS KEEPING WATCH OVER WAT PHRA KAEO.

156 - CHEDI PHRA SRI RATANA IS PART OF THE WAT PHRA KAEO COMPLEX.

157 - THE *PRANG* THAT DOMINATES WAT PICHAYART AT THONBURI.

# THE JEWEL OF THE GODS: THE ART OF BANGKOK

158 - A Ratanakosin-style statue (h. 34 in/ 88 cm) of Buddha adorned with royal insignia (Prasart Museum, Bangkok).

159 top - Ivory and gold are the components of this portrait of Buddha as Phra Chai or Lord of Victory (Prasart Museum, Bangkok).

159 bottom - Figures of praying worshippers stand out on the panels that decorate an elegant chest made during the Ratanakosin period (Musée Guimet, Paris).

The artistic activity during the Bangkok period is usually divided into two phases: the first includes the brief Thonburi period and continues up to 1851, while the second one begins with the reign of Rama IV (King Mongkut), who ascended the throne in 1851. The artistic production that flourished during the entire period is also known as 'Ratanakosin art,' a name that corresponds to the phase ranging from the ascension of Rama I almost to the mid-20th century. In no other epoch was art so closely identified with the activities promoted in the capital and financed by the royal family. They summoned artists, architects, sculptors and painters to court to undertake the revival of cultural life, which had been seriously jeopardized by the ruin of Ayutthaya. This desire to reestablish continuity with the past was expressed in various forms by the kings of the Chakri dynasty, who wanted to set themselves up as the heirs of the ancient Thai sovereigns and, at the same time, as the authors, in their role as universal monarchs, of a new age of prosperity. The measures taken to sanction this political and religious program were the transfer to the capital of the most venerated images and relics in the country. They also revived the royal ceremonies that had fallen into oblivion after the fall of Ayutthaya, and lastly, they reinstated the references and usage of 16th-18th century art, which became the stylistic hallmark of the first period.

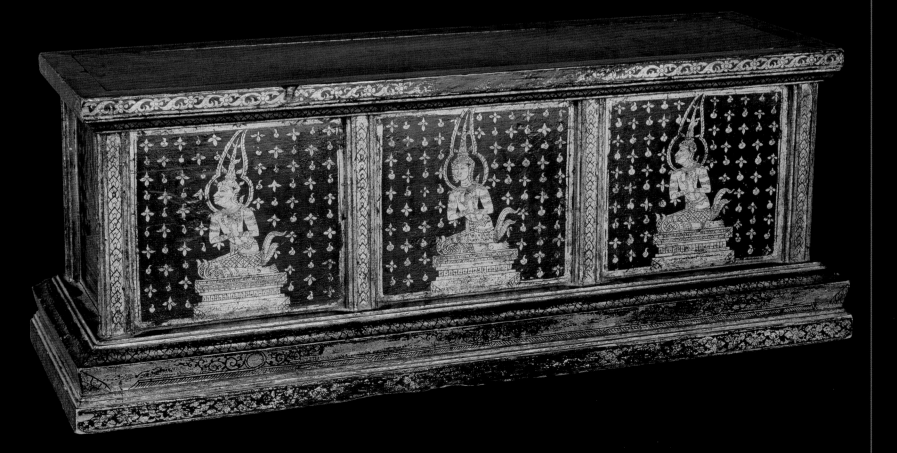

160-161 - A ROW OF *PRANGS* BORDERS THE EAST SIDE OF THE WAT PHRA KAEO COMPLEX IN BANGKOK. TO THE WEST OF THE FIRST TOWER AT LEFT IS THE BUILDING HOUSING THE EMERALD BUDDHA, PHRA KAEO. TO THE RIGHT IS THE PRASAT PHRA THEPIDON (THE ROYAL PANTHEON, BUILT BY KING RAMA IV), WHICH IS CROWNED BY A *PRANG*. THE PANTHEON WAS ORIGINALLY INTENDED TO HOUSE THE STATUE OF THE EMERALD BUDDHA, BUT IT PROVED TO BE TOO MODEST AN EDIFICE FOR THE CERIMONIES.

Architectural activity began with Wat Phra Kaeo (or Kaew), the monastery built in 1785 to house the palladium of the kingdom inside the vast Grand Palace complex of royal edifices that was begun by Rama I in the same period and enlarged by his successors. Like Wat Mahathat at Sukhothai and Wat Phra Si Sanphet at Ayutthaya, Wat Phra Kaeo is a royal temple that does not house a monastic community. The monastery is built around a rectangular wall-portico (*phra rabieng*) where two platforms support the main edifices in the complex. Unlike Ayutthaya, the arrangement of the buildings in the Bangkok monasteries does not correspond to a precise order that revolves around the reliquary (either a *stupa* or *prang*), but all the components now appear to be equally important within the sacred precinct. The *bots* and *wihans* are larger, but retain the main features of the late-Ayutthaya style, with tall walls and external columns that support the ends of the roofs, which are generally overlapping and not separated from one another as in northern architecture. Here they tend to be arranged symmetrically. This period also produced pavilion roofs. The roofing invariably consists of glazed orange tiles with yellow and green borders. On the one hand the edifices appear to be lighter compared to those of Ayutthaya thanks to the thinner walls, and on the other hand, their decoration now features new elements and materials. Stuccowork and

gilded lacquering frame the doors and windows – the latter replacing the slits common in the ancient period – as well as the pillars and tympana, creating a pleasant contrast with the whitewashed walls. In other cases even the walls are decorated, with marble, stained glass, glazed ceramics and fragments of mother-of-pearl. The increase in the proportions of the buildings can be clearly noted in the *bot* of Wat Phra Kaeo, the main edifice in the complex, built in 1785 to house the statue of the Emerald Buddha. The huge hall with an external colonnade rises on a marble platform and has three doors on the east side and three more on the west side. Situated around the base of the platform are the traditional eight *sima*, placed inside small pavilions in the shape of *mondops*. A stairway, guarded by stone lions, leads to the interior of the hall, at the end of which is a monumental altar dating from the time of King Rama III (1824-1851). Packed with intricate decoration and surrounded by numerous statues, the altar supports the small Emerald Buddha image. This statue is decorated with ornate attire that is changed three times a year, in compliance with a tradition that dates back to the Khmer custom of adorning the statues with real jewels. Likewise, the Emerald Buddha is covered with a monk's cloak during the rainy season, with royal attire during the hot season and with a mantle decorated with golden pearls during the cold season.

161 LEFT - A SEVEN-HEADED *NAGA* (SERPENT) IS SITUATED IN THE MIDDLE OF THE TYMPANUM OF A BUILDING IN WAT PHRA KAEO.

161 RIGHT - GIGANTIC STATUES OF *YAKHSA* GUARD THE MAIN ACCESSES TO WAT PHRA KAEO.

162 - A LARGE STATUE OF A *YAKHSA* WITH A BLUE COMPLEXION KEEPING GUARD OVER ONE OF THE ENTRANCES TO WAT PHRA KAEO. IT IS SAID THAT THESE BEINGS WERE INITIALLY HOSTILE TO BUDDHA AND HIS DOCTRINE, BUT LATER BECAME FORMIDABLE DEFENDERS OF BOTH.

163 - THE MONUMENTS AND TERRACES OF WAT PHRA KAEO ARE POPULATED WITH BEAUTIFUL STATUES OF HYBRID FEMALES (*KINNARI*) THAT ARE HALF-HUMAN AND HALF-BIRD. TOGETHER WITH OTHER DEMIGODS *KINNARI* FORM CELESTIAL ORCHESTRA.

164 - BESIDES BEING GUARDS, THE *YAKSHA* ALSO SERVE AS A SORT OF ATLAS, IN THIS CASE SUPPORTING THE TWO GILDED *CHEDI* ON A SQUARE BASE SITUATED EAST OF THE PRASAT PHRA THEPIDON, IN FRONT OF THE ENTRANCE TO THIS MONUMENT.

165 - A GUARDIAN DEMON WITH A STERN GLANCE, RESTING ON A LARGE MACE, STANDS IN FRONT OF THE LIBRARY OF SACRED WRITINGS, THE PHRA MONDOP, BUILT DURING THE REIGN OF KING RAMA I (1782-1809) IN THE WAT PHRA KAEO COMPLEX.

166-167 - THE FIGURE OF THE ADORING DIVINITY IN THE MIDDLE OF THE TYMPANUM OF A BUILDING IN WAT PHRA KAEO IS A CHARACTERISTIC MOTIF OF RATANAKOSIN ARCHITECTURE.

168 - A FIVE-HEADED GILDED *NAGA* DECORATES THE ENTRANCE STAIRWAY OF THE PHRA MONDOP.

169 - RATANAKOSIN ART USED A GREAT DEAL OF COLOR, WHICH ON MANY OCCASIONS WAS APPLIED IN THE FORM OF MOSAIC TESSERAE, WHICH OFTEN CONSISTED OF REFLECTING MATERIALS. THE 'GILDING' THAT COVERS THESE FIGURES OF DIVINE CREATURES WHO ARE PRAYING WAS OBTAINED FROM COPPER.

170-171 - ON THE PLATFORM OF THE *BOT* WHERE LIES THE EMERALD BUDDHA, THE BASE OF THE EDIFICE IS IDEALLY 'SUPPORTED' BY ROWS OF *GARUDA*.

172 TOP AND BOTTOM -
DURING SPECIAL CERIMONIES,
THE EMERALD BUDDHA IS
CLOTHED WITH DIFFERENT
ATTIRE DEPENDING ON THE
PERIOD OF THE YEAR.
IN THESE PHOTOGRAPHS
HE IS WEARING THE COLD
(TOP) AND WARM SEASON
(BOTTOM) CLOTHING.

172-173 - THE EMERALD
BUDDHA IS HOUSED IN A
*BOT* THAT HAS INCREDIBLY
LAVISH DECORATION.
IT IS THOUGHT THAT
THIS FAMOUS IMAGE HAS
GREAT MAGICAL POWERS
AND, THUS, IS REGARDED
AS THE PALLADIUM
OF THAILAND.

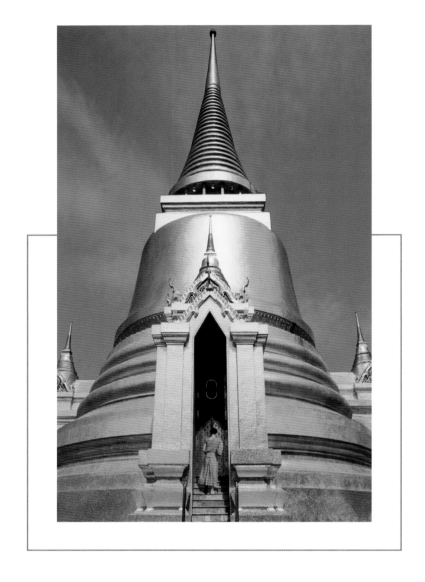

On a broad terrace next to the *bot* and starting off from the east, are the Prasat Phra Thepidon, the Phra Mondop and the Phra Si Ratana Chedi. The first monument is a cruciform structure that was built in 1855 to house the statues of the first kings of the Chakri dynasty but was rebuilt after a fire broke out in the early-20th century. A hallmark sign of the eclectic architecture of this epoch, the roof of the *prasada* is crowned by a tall *prang* that rises up from the junction of the roofs, and two gilded Ayutthaya-style *stupas* define the main entrance to the hall. The next building, a square *mondop* with a pyramidal roof that has a tapering spire, was built at the end of the 18th century and was used to house and preserve sacred texts. The series ends with the bell-shaped *stupa* adorned with gold leaf that imitates those in Wat Si Sanphet at Ayutthaya and like the latter, has four niches with avant-corps at the cardinal points. The long arcade that surrounds the monastery has retained the entire cycle of paintings with scenes from the *Ramayana*, which has always been one of the most popular themes, together with the *jataka*, the episodes from the life of Buddha and the themes of the encyclopedic *Traiphum*. The Wat Phra Kaeo cycle dates to the end of the 18th century, but it was renovated several times in the 19th and 20th centuries.

**174** - ENTIRELY DRESSED WITH GILDED LAYERS, THE BRILLIANT PHRA SI RATANA *CHEDI* IS THE FOCAL POINT OF THE WAT PHRA KAEO COMPLEX. IT WAS CONSTRUCTED BY KING RAMA IV, WHO USED IT TO HOUSE A HOLY RELIC OF BUDDHA.

**175** AND **176-177** - THE WALLS OF THE PORTICO ENCLOSING THE WAT PHRA KAEO COMPLEX ARE DECORATED WITH A SPLENDID SERIES OF SCENES FROM THE *RAMAKIEN*, THE THAI VERSION OF THE *RAMAYANA*, THE FAMOUS INDIAN EPIC POEM.

178-179 AND 179 - THE STYLE OF THE
WALL PAINTINGS INSPIRED BY THE
*RAMAKIEN* IN THE GALLERIES OF WAT
PHRA KAEO IS EXTREMELY VIVACIOUS
AND PERFECTLY IN THE SPIRIT OF THE
WORK ITSELF, WHICH IS 'LIGHTER' AND
MORE LIKE A FAIRY TALE THAN THE
ORIGINAL INDIAN WORK.
THE 178 PANELS ARE A VIVID
TESTIMONY OF THE DAILY LIFE AND
COURT CUSTOMS OF THE THONBURI
AND BANGKOK PERIOD.

180-181 - THE PICTORIAL CYCLE OF THE *RAMAKIEN* DATES TO THE LATE 18TH CENTURY, DURING THE REIGN OF KING RAMA I. HERE WE CAN RECOGNIZE ONE OF THE MOST POPULAR FIGURES IN THE ENTIRE CYCLE, HANUMAN, THE BENEVOLENT MONKEY GOD WHO HELPS RAMA TO LIBERATE HIS WIFE SITA FROM THE KING OF LANKA, RAVANA, WHO HAS ABDUCTED HER.

181 - THERE ARE TWO MAIN THEMES IN THE WAT PHRA KAEO PAINTINGS: THE STRUGGLE BETWEEN GOOD AND EVIL (BETWEEN THE HUMANS, WHOSE PALADIN IS RAMA, AND THE DEMONS LED BY TOSAKANTH), AND THE INCARNATIONS OF THE HERO RAMA BEFORE BECOMING PHRA RAM (LORD RAMA). THE PAINTINGS WERE RESTORED ON SPECIAL OCCASIONS, SUCH AS THE CELEBRATIONS FOR THE 150TH AND 200TH ANNIVERSARY OF THE FOUNDATION OF BANGKOK, IN 1932 AND 1982.

The royal monastery lies in the complex of the Grand Palace: construction began in 1785 and ended a century later. This site comprises the inner, outer and central parts of the precinct of Wat Phra Kaeo, thus following the layout and division of the royal palace of Ayutthaya. The inner section contained the buildings used as residences for the king's wives, daughters and concubines. The central section had the royal residence and audience halls, while the external one housed the government offices and royal treasury. The Dusit Maha Prasat group includes the structures built during the reign of Rama I, such as the throne hall (Phra Thinang Dusit Maha Prasat), which was rebuilt after a fire. This hall embodies in every aspect the symbolism of royal power that, over the centuries, attained perfection in Thai architecture. This is a large cruciform building with a crown in the shape of a pyram-

Wang Na, built at the site now occupied by the National Museum, north of the Grand Palace. The only remaining original building is the Putthaisawan Chapel, famous for the splendid wall paintings and for the statue of the Phra Phuttha Sihing that is kept on the main altar. The gilded bronze sculpture portraying the seated Buddha meditating was probably created in the early-15th century as a copy of the safeguard of Sukhothai. It was later transferred to Wat Pho in Bangkok, where it is still venerated as the second most important icon in the country. The large walls in the hall are decorated with four horizontal displays, with alternating black and red backgrounds and images of seated divinities adoring the Phra Phuttha Sihing, while the sections between the windows are occupied by large compositions containing episodes from the life of Buddha. The style of the paintings (1795-1797),

idal *chedi* recalling that of the analogous cruciform hall of Wat Si Sanphet at Ayutthaya. The construction of the elegant Aphon Phimok Prasat, a pavilion standing at the side of the throne hall and used by the kings to change their clothes before entering the royal palanquin, dates from a later period. The central sector also includes the Chakri Mahaprasat, the throne hall commissioned by Rama V (1868-1910). It was built in the eclectic style, with marked Western influences, which distinguished Thai architecture in the second half of the 19th century. The Neo-classical style, from which the English architect who built it drew inspiration, is overwhelmingly extravagant: the typical Thai-style roofs, utilized because they were considered symbolically more appropriate for the throne hall, do not fit in with the style of the building. The viceroy, the younger brother of King Rama I, had his palace, the

harks back to that of Ayutthaya, but has a wider gamut of colors. This includes the dark tones used for the backgrounds that consist of landscape scenes that are foreign to earlier painting styles. The classical tradition continued and reached its apogee during the reign of Rama III, who championed painting strongly: he commissioned the paintings on the columns of Wat Suthat, which illustrate some of the *jataka* and the edifying scenes inspired by the life of Buddha and other themes of Buddhist doctrine. These works covered all the available space of the Wat Pho *wihans* and *bots*. Another interesting painting collection is in the *bot* of Wat Suwannaram at Thonburi (early-19th century), whose iconographic agenda includes the popular theme of the last 'ten *jataka*' (*tosachat*), the episode of Buddha defeating Mara, and a composition inspired by Buddhist cosmography.

182 LEFT - WAT SUTHAT WAS BUILT
DURING THE REIGNS OF THREE KINGS.

182 RIGHT - THE CHAKRI MAHAPRASAT
SHOWS AN ECLECTIC STYLE.

183 - A THRONE IN THE SHAPE OF A BOAT
IS THE FOCAL POINT OF THE AMARINDA
VINICHAI HALL INSIDE THE GRAND
PALACE, WHERE THE FIRST KINGS OF THE
CHAKRI DYNASTY HELD AUDIENCE.

184-185 - Dozens of statues of Buddha are lined along the portico of Wat Suthat. This monastery has a very large *wihan* and *bot*, both of which are decorated with painting cycles dating from the time of King Rama III.

186 - The wall paintings in the Putthaisawan Chapel show episodes from the life of Buddha: here the Enlightened One descends from the heaven of the 33 gods by means of a triple stair.

187 - The narrative paintings in the Putthaisawan Chapel beautifully combine scenes from the life of Buddha and representations of everyday life in Thailand.

On the site of an ancient monastery built during the Ayutthaya period, King Rama I ordered the construction of a new complex at the end of the 18th century, Wat Pho (or Wat Phra Chetuphon), which was renovated by King Rama III. This is the largest complex in Bangkok and, on the occasion of this renovation and enlargement work, a center dedicated to the study of traditional culture was established. The front area of the *wat*, bounded by a rectangular enclosure wall, is occupied by a large *bot* that is delimited by another wall. This wall is punctuated by four *wihans* that serve as entrances and form two inner courts

on each of the four sides of the *bot* enclosure. There are 152 marble slab panels sculpted in low relief set around the base of the hall, each of which depicts a scene from the *Ramayana* and appear to date from the reign of Rama III. The same motif is used in the lacquered mother-of-pearl inlay decoration on the doors of the *bot*, which are considered to be one of the masterpieces of this art, which attained its acme in the Ayutthaya period and continued in the first Ratanakosin period. The western part of the complex includes four *chedis* that commemorate the first kings of the Chakri dynasty and a library flanked on both sides by a Chinese-style and a Western-style pavilion. Lastly, in the northwest corner of the monastery there is the *wihan* that Rama III commissioned to house a colossal stuccoed and gilded brick statue of a reclining Buddha. The feet of this gigantic work are a masterpiece in themselves: in deference to the tradition of the *buddhapada*, the soles are entirely decorated with a mother-of-pearl inlay that illustrates the 108 auspicious signs of good fortune.

188 - A CHAPEL ON A TALL BASE IS SITUATED IMMEDIATELY EAST OF WAT PHO'S *WIHAN*, THE INTERIOR OF WHICH IS ALMOST ENTIRELY OCCUPIED BY THE STATUE OF THE RECLINING BUDDHA.

188-189 - SOUTH OF WAT PHO'S *WIHAN*, RAMA III ORDERED TO BUILD PHRA MONDOP, THE HALL OF SACRED WRITINGS, WHICH IS DECORATED WITH CERAMIC FRAGMENTS INSERTED INTO THE STUCCO.

190 - WAT PHO OFFERS SOME OF THE BEST EXAMPLES OF THAI INLAY WORK, WHICH IS TO BE FOUND BOTH ON THE DOORS OF THE *WIHAN* AND ON THE SOLES OF THE RECLINING BUDDHA'S FEET. THE MOTHER-OF-PEARL, TAKEN FROM THE SHELLS BELONGING TO THE TURBINIDAE FAMILY, IS MOUNTED WITH INCREDIBLE METICULOUSNESS ONTO THE LACQUERED SURFACE.

190-191 - THE GILDED, 150 FT (46 M) LONG RECLINING BUDDHA WAS PLACED IN WAT PHO IN 1832, DURING THE REIGN OF RAMA III. DRESSED IN GOLD, THIS FAMOUS STATUE IS KNOWN ESPECIALLY FOR THE SOLES OF THE FEET, WHICH ARE DECORATED WITH 108 SIGNS OF GOOD OMEN WITH MOTHER-OF-PEARL INLAY.

On the site of Thonburi, on the opposite bank of the Chao Phraya River, is Wat Arun, the temple that in 1780 housed the Emerald Buddha statue until it was transferred to Wat Phra Kaeo. Later on the complex was altered during the reigns of Rama II and Rama III, who ordered the construction of the impressive *prang* – whose form was modeled on that of comparable *prangs* in Ayutthaya – that dominates the complex. Four other *prangs*, identical to the central one but smaller, are arranged at the corners of the platform and, like the main one, are entirely covered with painted stucco decoration and fragments of colored ceramics donated by worshippers. The monumental base of the *prang* is accessible by means of four stairways at the cardinal points, each of which is preceded by a pavilion (*mondop*) that contains an image drawn from the life of Buddha. On top of the tripartite base, at the end of the stairways, are niches containing statues of the god Indra on the three-headed elephant Airavata. A sumptuous architectural translation of Buddhist cosmology, the tripartite shape of the base of the *prang* reflects the three-fold division of the universe, while the host of figurines that cover every part of the monument represent the multitude of divine and semi-divine beings and demons that populate the world of reality.

192-193 - ONE OF THE MOST UNUSUAL THAI TEMPLES, WAT ARUN LIES ON THE RIGHT BANK OF THE CHAO PHRAYA, AT THONBURI, WHERE IT WAS BUILT AT THE BEGINNING OF THE 19TH CENTURY.

193 LEFT AND CENTER - A GILDED METAL CROWN TOPS THE NINE-LEVEL SPIRE OF THE CENTRAL *PRANG* OF WAT ARUN, WHOSE PRESENT APPEARANCE IS THE RESULT OF REBUILDING AND RESTORATION CARRIED OUT IN DIFFERENT PHASES.

193 RIGHT - FOUR SATELLITE *PRANGS* SURROUND THE MAIN MOUNTAIN TOWER OF WAT ARUN. THE NICHES CONTAIN EFFIGIES OF THE PHRA PHAI WIND GODS.

**194** AND **196-197** - ROWS OF MYTHOLOGICAL BEINGS IDEALLY SUPPORT THE CENTRAL *PRANG* OF WAT ARUN. THEY, TOO, ARE DECORATED WITH CERAMIC FRAGMENTS THAT FOR THE MOST PART WERE DONATED BY THE FAITHFUL.

**195** - ONLY THROUGH CLOSE-UP OBSERVATION CAN ONE REALIZE HOW MUCH PAINSTAKING WORK WENT INTO THE DECORATION OF THE WAT ARUN *PRANG*, WHICH CONSISTS OF CERAMIC FRAGMENTS AND TESSERAE APPLIED TO THE STUCCO.

The reign of Rama III heralded the vogue of Chinese architecture, which spread in the second half of the 19th century, preceding the popularity of Westernizing buildings by a few years. This predilection for Chinese taste was expressed mainly in *wats* built in the Thonburi area – Wat Ratchaorot and Wat Thong Nophakhun – in which the shape of the roofs, the ceramic decoration, the wall paintings and other details recall a renewal of interest in, rather than an actual imitation of, the Chinese style. In the second half of the 19th century, during the reign of Rama IV (1851-1868), architectural tastes took a new turn. The search for an innovative direction and the new receptive attitude toward outside influences led to an eclectic style in both religious and civil architecture, which consisted of combining edifices modeled on different traditions within the same complex. This led to the construction, in 1864, of Wat Ratchapradit, in which the multiplicity of models can be noted in the variety of building materials employed and the many types of edifices constructed there. In fact, this complex comprises a Thai *bot*

made of Chinese marble, a Singhalese-type *stupa*, a *prang*, and a building that recalls the Bayon style featured at Angkor Thom. The change in artistic taste promoted by King Mongkut also concerned painting, which now began to make use of Western perspectives and three-dimensional rendering. The painter Khrua In Khong was the facilitator of this period of experimentation. The new art marked the abandonment of the classical tradition in favor of an unusual mode that merges elements of Western painting and components typical of the local tradition. The king commissioned Khrua In Khong to decorate the inside walls of the *bot* in Wat Bovornivet, which was

built in 1827. He created the traditional motifs of Buddhist paintings and depicted them in fantastic settings and landscapes, carefully rendering every detail and constructing the final result with tonal and chiaroscuro (three-dimensional) effects. Khrua In Khong's new painting style resulted in the formation of a school that operated parallel to traditional Thai painting. The use of marble, fragments of ceramics and stained glass adds a touch of refinement to the animated configuration of Wat Ratchabopit, a complex built during the reign of Rama V that has an almost Baroque quality to it. The pivotal point of the monastery is the monumental *chedi* built in the Singhalese style, around which are three *wihans* and one *bot,* joined by segmented arches in the wall-gallery that outline the complex. The interior of the *bot* also seems to be alien to traditional Thai edifices, since it is decorated in a style that merges various Western traditions in a condensed manner. Of particular interest are the panels on the doors and windows of the *bot,* which reproduce the royal insignia, offering one of the most sumptuous examples of gilded black lacquer decoration and mother-of-pearl inlay. But more than any other building, it is perhaps the summer palace known as Bang Pa In that best embodies the kings' predilection for the combination of Eastern and Western elements. The residence, which is situated a short distance from Ayutthaya, was built in the mid-17th century, but after being abandoned for a certain time was again used by King Mongkut and his successor, Rama V, who added new structures to it. Indeed, inside the complex there is an alternation to the pavilion on the water in the Thai style, edifices built in the Neo-classical style, Khmer-inspired towers, and Chinese-style palaces.

200 and 201 - Wehart Chamrun was built inside the Bang Pa In residence at the end of the 19th century thanks to the initiative of the Chinese Chamber of Commerce, which realized a revival, so to speak, of the lavish decorative qualities of architecture that prevailed when the power of the Celestial Empire was in decline. More than the overall work, what can be appreciated most are the details, which were executed with extreme and masterful precision, through the use of excellent and unusual materials such as camel bone.

202 - A sort of royal *divertissement* (because King Rama V commissioned it) can be noted in the lavish Chinese-style decoration in the Wehart Chamrun, one of the edifices of the summer royal palace complex of Bang Pa In.

202-203 - The island on Chao Phraya, which now houses Wehart Chamrung and the other buildings of Bang Pa In, was the home of the royal palace built by King Prasat Thong of Ayutthaya in 1632. It was abandoned after the city was destroyed in 1767 and then resurrected thanks to the first restoration work carried out by King Rama IV in the mid-19th century.

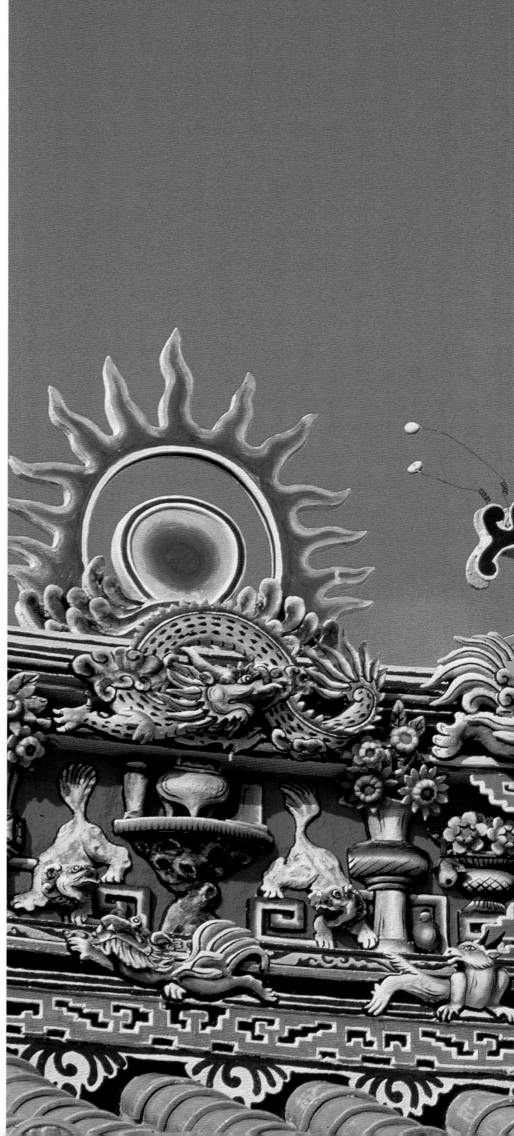

# GLOSSARY

*The abbreviations in brackets indicate that the term is Sanskrit (s.), Thai (t.), Pali (p.) or Khmer (k.).*
*The Sanskrit and Pali terms are transcribed with the conventional diacritical marks.*

**abhayamudrā**: (s.) the open hand gesture with the palm facing outward to indicate reassurance.

**añjalimudrā**: (s.) gesture made with the hands joined as a sign of veneration.

**arūpaloka**: (s.) in Buddhist cosmology, the "world without form."

**bhūmisparśamudrā**: (s.) the gesture made by Buddha with his right hand to summon the Earth to testify that he has attained enlightenment.

**bodhisattva**: (s.) in Buddhism, the state of those who, having attained enlightenment, forego *nirvana* in order to help others to achieve liberation.

**bot**: (t.) the Thai abbreviation for *ubosoth.*

**buddhavāsa**: (s.) *putthawat* in Thai. The sacred area inside which is the monastic complex, bounded by an enclosure wall that sometimes opens onto an arcade (*phra rabieng*).

**caitya**: (s.) in Indian culture, a place of worship; Buddhists often identify it with the *stupa.*

**chedi**: (t.) term derived from the Pali word *cetiya*, the equivalent of the Sanskrit term *caitya*, indicating a monument used as a reliquary.

**cho fa**: (t.) a hooked element placed at the ends of the ridge beam of the *bot, wihan* and minor rooms.

**devarāja**: (s.) "the god who is king," a term used by the Khmer to indicate the basic identification of the sovereign with the supreme divinity.

**dharmacakra**: (s.) "the wheel of the Law," the symbolic representation of Buddhist Law (Dharma) by means of a wheel.

**dharmacakrastambha**: (s.) "pillar of the wheel," a Buddhist monument consisting of a wheel – the representation of the Dharma – set on top of a sculpted pillar.

**dharmacakramudrā**: (s.) a gesture made by Buddha with both hands that indicates the exposition of Buddhist Law, that is, setting the "Wheel of the Law" in motion.

**dharmasala**: (s.) buildings used to house pilgrims.

**dhyānamudrā**: (s.) the position of the hands on one's lap, one over the other, with the palms facing upward to indicate the state of concentration while in meditation.

**gopura**: (s.) in Indian architecture and the schools that derived from it, the portal or entrance pavilion of the temple, characterized by a solemn pitched roof.

**harmikā**: (s.) an architectural element similar to an enclosure that lies on the top of the *stupa.*

**ho trai**: (t.) a library, or small structure, somewhat elevated from ground level that lies inside the monastery complex and is used to preserve Buddhist writings.

**jātaka**: (s.) stories narrating the previous births of Buddha.

**kāmaloka**: (s.) the "world of craving" that in Buddhist cosmology corresponds to the world of manifestation.

**kong khieu**: (t.) a wooden cornice in the shape of the eyebrow arch that closes off the space between the central and side columns of the façade of the *bot* and *wihan.*

**ku**: (t.) a monumental altar in the shape of a temple mountain placed at the end of the *wihan*, where the image of Buddha is also situated.

**lak muang**: (t.) a column placed in the geometric center of Thai cities in the vicinity of the royal palace.

**lakṣaṇa**: (s.) physical features that allude to the extraordinary nature of Buddha.

**linga**: (s.) a sculpture in the shape of a phallus that symbolically represents the god Shiva.

**luk nimit**: (t.) spheres buried outside the *ubosoth* in correspondence with the four cardinal points and the four intermediate ones to delimit the sacred area.

**mandala**: (s.) "circle." A geometric diagram used as an instrument for meditation or as a model for the construction of temples that reflect the geometric representation of the Universe. In a wider sense this term indicates the political entities or states that rose up in Southeast Asia.

**mandapa**: (s.) a term in Indian architecture for a columned hall in the temple.

**mondop**: (t.) the Thai word for *mandapa*, but different from the Indian model from an architectural standpoint.

**muang**: (t.) a city-state.

**nāga**: (s.) "serpent." In Indian mythology, semi-divine beings with the body of a serpent and a human face, the lords of the underground and underwater worlds.

**nāgarāja**: (s.) "king of the *nagas.*"

**nirvāṇa**: (s.) in Buddhist thought, the state of liberation from the birth-death-rebirth cycle.

**phra attharot**: (t.) a colossal statue of Buddha 27 ft (8.5 m) high.

**phra rabieng**: (t.) the cloister that surrounds one or more edifices in the *wat.*

**pradakṣiṇa**: (s.) the circumambulatory ritual that is performed clockwise in the sacred monuments.

**pralambapādāsana**: (s.) a seated position with the feet on the ground, also known as the "European" position.

**prang**: (t.) the reliquary tower typical of Thai architecture (especially that of Ayutthaya) which consists of a cubic cell on a tall platform and is surrounded by a rather tall and streamlined spire.

**prāsāda**: (s.) a term in Indian architecture for the temple, here indicating the secular buildings used by the members of the royal family.

**prasat**: (k.) in Khmer architecture, the word for the sanctuary or temple, consisting of a cubic cell surmounted by a roof with superposed levels of decreasing size.

**pyhatthat**: Burmese word for the wooden pavilions with multiple roofs that crown the entrances or important edifices.

**ratna-cetiya**: (p.) "*stupa*-jewel." This word indicates a particular type of *stupa* of unknown origin that was widespread in Lan Na.

**rūpaloka**: (s.) the world of forms.

**sala**: (t.) an open pavilion situated inside the *wat.*

**samsāra**: (s.) the cycle of birth, death and rebirth.

**sattaphan**: (t.) an elaborate candelabrum near the altar inside the *wihan.*

**sima**: (t.) sculpted stones or stelae placed in correspondence with the eight points that delimit the sacred space around the *ubosoth*. The ninth point is situated on a level with the altar. See *luk nimit.*

**Śrī**: the Indian goddess of prosperity and abundance.

**stūpa**: (s.) the reliquary used to house the ashes of Buddha, in a later period transformed into a commemorative symbol and principal monument of the Buddhist world.

**Sūrya**: the Indian sun god.

**thammat**: (t.) pulpit inside the *wihan*, next to the altar (*ku*).

**uposathaghara**: (p.) the hall in a Buddhist monastery used by the monastic community for religious practices and the ordination of the monks.

**ubosoth**: (t.) the Thai term for the Pali word *uposathaghara*

**ūrṇā**: the protuberance (or cluster of hairs) between the Buddha's eyebrows.

**ūṣṇīṣa**: (s.) a cranial protuberance, one of the Buddha's *lakshana*, represented in different manners by the various schools of Buddhist art.

**vajrāsana**: (s.) a seated position with the legs crossed and both soles of the feet facing upward.

**varadamudrā**: (s.) a gesture made with the outstretched hand, the palm facing upward as a sign of offering.

**vihāra**: (s.) a Buddhist monastery.

**virāsana**: (s.) a seated position similar to the *vajrasana* but with the right leg crossed over the left one so that only the sole of the right foot is visible.

**Viṣṇu**: one of the supreme Hindu gods.

**vitarkamudrā**: (s.) a gesture made with the hand, with the forefinger and thumb curved and touching one another, while the other fingers are barely bent. This is the teaching gesture.

**wat**: (t.) a Buddhist complex bounded by an enclosure wall and comprising worship structures and, in some cases, lodgings for the monks as well.

**wiang**: (t.) a fortified settlement.

**wihan**: (t.) the Thai word corresponding to *vihara*. It stands for the hall containing the main religious image that is used for communal prayers and for ordaining the novices.

**yakṣa**: in Indian mythology, the spirit of nature that often acts as the guardian of a site.

# INDEX

Aung Thaw, *Historical Sites in Burma*. Ministry of Union Culture, Government of the Union of Burma, 1972.
Bechert, H. & Gombrich, R. (ed.), *The World of Buddhism*. London, Thames and Hudson, 1984.
Boisselier, J. & Beurdeley, J.-M., *La sculpture en Thailande*. Fribourg, Office du livre, 1974.
Boisselier, J., *The Heritage of Thai Sculpture*. New York, Weatherhill, 1975.
Boisselier, J., *Il Sud-Est asiatico*. Turin, Utet, 1986.
Bowie, T.H., *The Sculpture of Thailand*. New York, The Asia Society, 1972.
Brown, R. L., *The Dvaravati Wheels of the Law and the Indianization of South East Asia*. Leiden, Brill, 1995.
Brown, R. L. (ed.), *Art from Thailand*. Mumbai, Marg Pubs., 1999.
Carrithers, M., *The Buddha: A Very Short Introduction*. Oxford-New York, Oxford University Press, 2001
Ciarla, R. & Rispoli, F., *Ceramiche e bronzi dall'Oriente Estremo*. Rome, Museo Nazionale d'Arte Orientale, 1999.
Coomaraswamy, A. K., *History of Indian and Indonesian Art*. New York, Dover Publications, 1985 (1927).
Dumarçay, J. & Smithies, M., *Cultural Sites of Burma, Thailand, and Cambodia*. Kuala Lumpur, Oxford University Press, 1995.
Fickle, D.H., *Images of the Buddha in Thailand*. Singapore, Oxford University Press, 1989.
Filoramo, G. (ed.), *Religioni dell'India e dell'Estremo Oriente*, in 'Storia delle Religioni.' Bari, Laterza, 1996.
Fontein, J. (ed.), *Bouddhas du Siam. Trésors du Royaume de Thaïlande*. Bruxelles, Snoeck-Ducaju & Zoon, 1997.
Franci, G. R., *Il buddhismo*. Bologna, Il Mulino, 2004.
Freeman, M., *A Guide to Khmer Temples in Thailand and Laos*. Bangkok, River Books, 1996.
Freeman, M., *Lanna. Thailand's Northern Kingdom*. London, Thames & Hudson, 2001.
Garnier, D., *Ayutthaya. Venice of the East*. Bangkok, River Books, 2004.
Giteau, M., *Les Khmers. Sculptures Khmères reflects de la civilisation d'Angkor*. Fribourg, 1965.
Gosling, B., *Origins of Thai Art*. Bangkok, River Books, 2004.
Green, A. & Blurton, T. R., *Burma. Art and Archaeology*. London, The British Museum Press, 2002.
Griswold, A.B., *Dated Buddha Images of Northern Siam*. Ascona, Artibus Asiae Pubs., 1957.
Hall, D.G.E.A., *A History of South-East Asia*. London, Macmillan, 1958.
Higham, C.F.W., *The Archaeology of Mailand Southeast Asia*. Cambridge, Cambridge University Press, 1991 (1989).
Higham, C.F.W. & Thosarat, R., *Prehistoric Thailand*. Bangkok, River Books, 1998.
Huntington, S. L., *The Art of Ancient India*. New York-Tokyo, Weatherhill, 1985.
Jacques, C. & Freeman, M., *Angkor, cité khmer*. Bangkok, River Books, 2000.
Karow, O., *Burmese Buddhist Sculpture*. Bangkok, White Lotus, 1991.
Lyons, E., *Thai Traditional Painting, Bangkok*. Thailand Fine Arts Department, 1968.
McGill, F. (ed.), *The Kingdom of Siam*. Chicago-Ghent-Bangkok, Asian Art Museum-Snoeck Pubs.-Buppha Press, 2005.
Mazzeo, D. & Silvi Antonini, C., *Civiltà khmer*. Milan, Mondadori, 1972.
Mouhot, H., *Voyage dans les royaumes de Siam, de Cambodge, de Laos et autres parties centrales de l'Indo-Chine, 1858-1861*. Paris, 1863.
Naengnoi Suksri, *The Grand Palace. Bangkok*. London, Thames and Hudson, 1999.
O'Connor, S. Jr., *Hindu Gods of Peninsular Siam*. Ascona, Artibus Asiae Pubs., 1972.
Piriya Krairiksh, *Art Styles in Thailand*. Bangkok, Fine Arts Department, 1977.
Piriya Krairiksh, *Art in Peninsular Thailand prior to the Fourteenth Century A.D.* Bangkok, The Fine Arts Department, 1980.
Quaritch Wales, H. G., *Dvaravati, The Earliest Kingdom in Siam*. London, 1969.
Rawson, P., *The Art of Southeast Asia*. London, Thames & Hudson, 1990 (1967).
Sivaramamurti, C., 2 vols, *India, Ceylon, Nepal, Tibet*. Turin, Utet, 1988.
Smitthi Siribhadra & Moore, E., *Palaces of the Gods: Khmer Art & Architecture in Thailand*. Bangkok, River Books, 1992.
Strachan, P., *Pagan. Art and Architecture of Old Burma*. Arran, Scotland, Kiscadale Publications, 1989.
Stratton, C., *Buddhist Sculpture of Northern Thailand*. Chiang Mai, Silkworm Books, 2004.
Stratton, C. & McNair Scott, M., *The Art of Sukhothai*. Kuala Lumpur, Oxford University Press, 1981.
Subhadradis Diskul, M.C., *Thailande*, in 'Archaeologia Mundi.' Geneva, Nagel, 1976.
Subhadradis Diskul, M.C., *Sukhothai Art*. Bangkok, Thai Watana Panich Press, 1978.
Subhadradis Diskul, M.C., *The Art of Shrivijaya*. Oxford, Oxford University Press, 1980.
Subhadradis Diskul, M.C., *Hindu Gods At Sukhodaya*. Bangkok, White Lotus, 1990.
Sukhasvasti, S., Moore, E., & Stott, Ph., *Ancient Capitals of Thailand*. London, Thames & Hudson, 1996.
Swann, W., *Lost Cities of Asia. Ceylon Pagan Angkor*. London, Elek Books, 1966.
Swearer, Donald K., *The Buddhist World of Southeast Asia*. Albany, State University of New York Press, 1995.
Van Beek, S., & Invernizzi Tettoni, L., *The Arts of Thailand*. Singapore, Periplus, 2000 (1985).
Williams, P., *Buddhist Thought. A Complete Introduction to the Indian Tradition*. London-New York, Routledge, 2000.
Wray, E., Rosenfield, C. & Bailey, D., *Ten Lives of the Buddha*. New York-Tokyo, Weatherhill, 1996 (1972).
Wyatt, D.K., *Thailand: A Short History*. New Haven, Yale University Press, 1984.

Page 1 Livio Bourbon/Archivio White Star
Pages 2-3 John Everingham/Artasia
Pages 4-5 Getty Images
Page 6 Luca I. Tettoni/Corbis
Page 9 Luca I. Tettoni/Corbis
Pages 10-11 Luca I. Tettoni/Corbis
Page 12 Elisabetta Ferrero/Archivio White Star
Pages 14-15 Bruno Barbier/Hemis.fr
Pages 16-17 Yann Arthus-Bertrand/Corbis
Page 19 Thierry Ollivier/Photo RMN
Page 20 left Robert McLeod/Lantern Photography
Page 20 right Robert McLeod/Lantern Photography
Page 21 Arthur M. Sackler Galler, Smithsonian Institution, Washington, D.C., S2004.14
Page 23 Luca I. Tettoni/Corbis
Page 24 Luca I. Tettoni/Corbis
Page 25 Luca I. Tettoni/Corbis
Page 27 Luca I. Tettoni/Corbis
Page 28 Luca I. Tettoni/Corbis
Page 29 John Everingham/Artasia
Page 30 Luca I. Tettoni/Corbis
Page 31 Richard Lambert/Photo RMN
Page 32 Luca I. Tettoni/Corbis
Page 33 Richard Lambert/Photo RMN
Page 34 Luca I. Tettoni/Corbis
Page 36 Livio Bourbon/Archivio White Star
Page 37 left Livio Bourbon/Archivio White Star
Page 37 right Livio Bourbon/Archivio White Star
Pages 38-39 John Everingham/Artasia
Page 40 Luca I. Tettoni/Corbis
Page 41 Michael Freeman/Corbis
Page 42 Luca I. Tettoni/Corbis
Page 43 Michael Freeman
Page 44 Livio Bourbon/Archivio White Star
Page 46 Michael Freeman/Corbis
Page 47 Luca I. Tettoni
Pages 48-49 Antonio Attini/Archivio White Star
Pages 50-51 Antonio Attini/Archivio White Star
Page 52 Livio Bourbon/Archivio White Star
Page 53 Livio Bourbon/Archivio White Star
Page 55 Alamy Images
Page 56 left Thierry Ollivier/Photo RMN
Page 56 right Michael Freeman/Corbis
Page 57 Michael Freeman
Pages 58-59 Yann Arthus-Bertrand/Corbis
Page 59 Yann Arthus-Bertrand/Corbis
Pages 60-61 Livio Bourbon/Archivio White Star
Page 61 top Livio Bourbon/Archivio White Star
Page 61 bottom Livio Bourbon/Archivio White Star
Page 62 Livio Bourbon/Archivio White Star
Pages 62-63 Yann Arthus-Bertrand/Corbis
Page 64 Livio Bourbon/Archivio White Star
Page 65 top left Livio Bourbon/Archivio White Star
Page 65 top right Livio Bourbon/Archivio White Star
Page 65 bottom Livio Bourbon/Archivio White Star
Page 66 Livio Bourbon/Archivio White Star
Page 67 Livio Bourbon/Archivio White Star
Page 68 Livio Bourbon/Archivio White Star
Pages 68-69 Franck Guiziou/Hemis.fr
Page 69 top Livio Bourbon/Archivio White Star
Page 69 bottom Livio Bourbon/Archivio White Star
Page 70 top left Livio Bourbon/Archivio White Star
Page 70 top right Livio Bourbon/Archivio White Star
Page 70 bottom Luca I. Tettoni/Corbis
Page 71 Livio Bourbon/Archivio White Star
Page 72 Livio Bourbon/Archivio White Star
Page 73 top Livio Bourbon/Archivio White Star
Page 73 bottom Livio Bourbon/Archivio White Star
Page 75 Franck Guiziou/Hemis.fr
Page 76 Luca I. Tettoni/Corbis
Page 77 Luca I. Tettoni/Corbis
Page 78 left Michael Freeman

Page 78 right Michael Freeman
Page 79 Michael Freeman
Page 80 Bpk/Archivio Scala
Page 81 Bpk/Archivio Scala
Page 82 Bpk/Archivio Scala
Page 83 top Bpk/Archivio Scala
Page 83 bottom Bpk/Archivio Scala
Pages 84-85 Luca I. Tettoni/Corbis
Page 86 Alamy Images
Page 87 Livio Bourbon/Archivio White Star
Page 88 Michael Freeman/Corbis
Page 89 Luca I. Tettoni/Corbis
Page 90 Michael Freeman/Corbis
Page 91 Daniel Arnaudet/Photo RMN
Page 92 Thierry Ollivier/Photo RMN
Page 93 Luca I. Tettoni/Corbis
Pages 94-95 Artasia
Page 95 Luca I. Tettoni/Corbis
Page 96 Livio Bourbon/Archivio White Star
Pages 96-97 Livio Bourbon/Archivio White Star
Page 97 Livio Bourbon/Archivio White Star
Pages 98-99 Livio Bourbon/Archivio White Star
Page 99 top Livio Bourbon/Archivio White Star
Page 99 bottom Luca I. Tettoni/Corbis
Page 101 Romain Cintract/Hemis.fr
Page 102 Livio Bourbon/Archivio White Star
Page 103 Livio Bourbon/Archivio White Star
Page 104 Luca I. Tettoni/Corbis
Pages 104-105 Luca I. Tettoni/Corbis
Page 106 left Ayutthaya National Museum/Photobank
Page 106 right Ayutthaya National Museum/Photobank
Page 107 Ayutthaya National Museum/Photobank
Pages 108-109 Ayutthaya National Museum/Photobank
Page 109 Luca I. Tettoni
Page 110 top Luca I. Tettoni
Page 110 left Luca I. Tettoni
Page 110 right Luca I. Tettoni
Page 111 top Luca I. Tettoni
Page 111 center Luca I. Tettoni
Page 111 bottom Luca I. Tettoni
Page 112 Luca I. Tettoni
Page 113 Luca I. Tettoni
Page 114 Michael Freeman
Pages 114-115 Yann Arthus-Bertrand/Corbis
Page 116 Livio Bourbon/Archivio White Star
Pages 116-117 Yann Arthus-Bertrand/Corbis
Pages 118-119 Luca I. Tettoni/Corbis
Pages 120-121 Luca I. Tettoni/Corbis
Page 121 Luca I. Tettoni/Corbis
Page 122 Luca I. Tettoni/Corbis
Page 123 Luca I. Tettoni/Corbis
Page 124 Livio Bourbon/Archivio White Star
Page 125 Livio Bourbon/Archivio White Star
Page 126 left Livio Bourbon/Archivio White Star
Page 126 right Livio Bourbon/Archivio White Star
Page 128 top Livio Bourbon/Archivio White Star
Page 128 bottom left Livio Bourbon/Archivio White Star
Page 128 bottom right Livio Bourbon/Archivio White Star
Page 129 Livio Bourbon/Archivio White Star
Pages 130-131 Livio Bourbon/Archivio White Star
Page 131 Livio Bourbon/Archivio White Star
Page 132 Luca I. Tettoni/Corbis
Page 133 Luca I. Tettoni/Corbis
Page 134 Livio Bourbon/Archivio White Star
Page 135 Luca I. Tettoni/Corbis
Pages 136-137 Livio Bourbon/Archivio White Star
Page 138 Michael Freeman
Page 139 Michael Freeman
Page 140 Livio Bourbon/Archivio White Star
Page 141 left Livio Bourbon/Archivio White Star
Page 141 right Livio Bourbon/Archivio White Star

Page 142 top Michael Freeman
Page 142 center Michael Freeman
Page 142 bottom Michael Freeman
Page 143 Michael Freeman/Corbis
Pages 144-145 Franck Guiziou/Hemis.fr
Page 146 top Michael Freeman/Corbis
Page 146 bottom Roman Soumar/Corbis
Pages 146-147 Luca I. Tettoni/Corbis
Page 148 Akg-Images/Photoservice Electa
Page 149 Akg-Images/Photoservice Electa
Pages 150-151 Jeremy Horner/Corbis
Page 151 left Livio Bourbon/Archivio White Star
Page 151 right Livio Bourbon/Archivio White Star
Page 152 top Livio Bourbon/Archivio White Star
Page 152 bottom Livio Bourbon/Archivio White Star
Pages 152-153 Livio Bourbon/Archivio White Star
Page 154 Marcello Bertinetti/Archivio White Star
Page 156 Livio Bourbon/Archivio White Star
Page 157 John Everingham/Artasia
Page 158 Luca I. Tettoni/Corbis
Page 159 top Luca I. Tettoni/Corbis
Page 159 bottom Thierry Ollivier/Photo RMN
Pages 160-161 John Everingham/Artasia
Page 161 left Redlink/Corbis
Page 161 right Marcello Bertinetti/Archivio White Star
Page 162 Marcello Bertinetti/Archivio White Star
Page 163 Christophe Boisvieux
Page 164 John Everingham/Artasia
Page 165 John Everingham/Artasia
Pages 166-167 Marcello Bertinetti/Archivio White Star
Page 168 Paul C. Pet/zefa/Corbis
Page 169 Christophe Boisvieux/Corbis
Pages 170-171 Marcello Bertinetti/Archivio White Star
Page 172 top Michael Freeman
Page 172 bottom Michael Freeman
Pages 172-173 Luca I. Tettoni
Page 174 Alamy Images
Page 175 Archivio Alinari, Firenze
Pages 176-177 Archivio Alinari, Firenze
Pages 178-179 John Everingham/Artasia
Page 179 top Akg-Images/Photoservice Electa
Page 179 bottom Mireille Vautier/The Art Archive
Pages 180-181 Peerapong Prasutr
Page 181 top David Henley/CPA
Page 182 left Luca I. Tettoni/Corbis
Page 182 right Luca I. Tettoni
Page 183 Luca I. Tettoni
Pages 184-185 Christophe Boisvieux/Corbis
Page 186 Luca I. Tettoni/Corbis
Page 187 Luca I. Tettoni/Corbis
Page 188 Livio Bourbon/Archivio White Star
Pages 188-189 John Everingham/Artasia
Page 190 top Lindsay Hebberd/Corbis
Page 190 bottom Michael Freeman/Corbis
Pages 190-191 Livio Bourbon/Archivio White Star
Pages 192-193 Yann Arthus-Bertrand/Corbis
Page 193 top left Livio Bourbon/Archivio White Star
Page 193 top right Livio Bourbon/Archivio White Star
Page 193 bottom Livio Bourbon/Archivio White Star
Page 194 Livio Bourbon/Archivio White Star
Page 195 John Everingham/Artasia
Pages 196-197 Yang Liu/Corbis
Page 198 Michael Freeman/Corbis
Page 199 Luca I. Tettoni/Corbis
Page 200 Michael Freeman/Corbis
Page 201 Michael Freeman
Page 202 Michael Freeman/Corbis
Pages 202-203 Michael Freeman/Corbis
Page 208 Livio Bourbon/Archivio White Star

208 - THIS SEMI-DIVINE WOODEN FIGURINE IS A DECORATIVE ELEMENT AT WAT PHRA THAT LAMPANG LUANG. THE USE OF WOOD IS ONE OF THE CHARACTERISTIC FEATURES OF LAN NA ARCHITECTURE.